WILD
WISDOM

WILD
WISDOM

Zen Masters, Mountain Monks,
and Rebellious Eccentrics
Reflect on the Healing Power of Nature

EDITED BY
NEIL DOUGLAS-KLOTZ

FOREWORD BY
M. AMOS CLIFFORD

Cover and text design by Kathryn Sky-Peck
Cover "Tibet," 1936 by Nicholas Roerich,
Tretyakov Gallery, Moscow, Russia/Bridgeman Images
Typeset in Weiss

Excerpts by Rachel Carson from *Lost Woods: The Discovered Writing
of Rachel Carson.* Copyright © 1998 by Roger Allen Christie.
Reprinted by permission of Frances Collin, Trustee.

Hampton Roads Publishing Company, Inc.
Charlottesville, VA 22906
Distributed by Red Wheel/Weiser, LLC
www.redwheelweiser.com

Sign up for our newsletter and special offers by going to
www.redwheelweiser.com/newsletter.

ISBN: 978-1-64297-008-1

Library of Congress Cataloging-in-Publication Data available upon request.

Printed in the United States of America
M&G

10 9 8 7 6 5 4 3 2 1

The work of souls is by those inaudible words of the earth.
The earth does not withhold, it is generous enough.
The truths of the earth continually wait,
they are not so concealed either.
They are calm, subtle, intransmissible by print.

—WALT WHITMAN, from *The Real Words*

CONTENTS

FOREWORD

Two decades ago, while perusing the library of a small Zen center in California, I came across a Chinese text from the 10th or 11th century in which the Master instructed his disciples to choose a wild place to meditate. The type of place they chose mattered; it depended upon the disposition of the meditator and what barriers along their path were ripe for shattering. My memory (an unreliable instrument) holds his teachings thus: forests are a place for those who have not yet understood the interbeing of all things; rivers are for those who are rigid in their thinking, unable to discern how understanding flows through many states. Mountains, with their vistas and exposure to the weather, are for those whose egos are inflated in a way that prevents them from seeing beyond the narrow stories of their own wisdom. Deserts brought into vivid awareness the great matters of life and death.

Choosing the right kind of place for contemplation is an important matter on the journey toward wholeness. Sustained, intimate connection with nature is essential. These ideas inspired me to start a project I called "Coyote Zendo." I periodically chose a place in a wild setting and invited others to join me there for meditation. Away from the still halls of the temple, with its characteristic aroma of incense and the iconography of sacred images, another mind came forward. The trees and winds and shy creatures slowly emerged as the living manifestation of the Great Matter. As much I loved the temple, like the Buddha it was among the wild places that at last the world cracked open for me.

Twice I've returned to that library seeking the text. I wanted to make sure I remembered it correctly, but my efforts have been fruitless—I cannot find it, nor can I remember the author's name. Yet those pages have taken a mythic place in my mind as a kind of "lost manuscript" of great power. I have felt this as a loss and have regretted that I might never find these teachings again.

Until I read this volume.

The contents are organized in the ancient way of that Chinese master. Voices that speak from across the centuries are those of the forest, the waters, the mountains, and the desert. *The teachings are in here,* I realized I as savored each page. Each selection spoke to me. Again, and again I felt *seen* with a gaze turned to words deftly said. The selection on each page is an expression of wholeness and within that wholeness, there is always one particular line that pierces me, like an *arrow to the heart*. We are seen by such an arrow, and opened by it, so that we may see more.

If I may be so bold as to suggest a way to read (and be read by) this book it would be this: as you enter the pages, set notions of time aside. Declare it to be so, that clocks don't signify. Without seeking, let the words of these teachers seep into your body. Notice which phrases are your particular arrows to the heart. Let each of these piercings ripen, let them open a bleeding of your spirit onto the land, and let the land reach back into your heart. You don't have to figure out what it means. Let the intelligence of your whole living body *simply know*. Notice where in your body you are pierced; for the heart is not just a physical organ located in a singular space, but when we are in accord with our own nature, there is something of the heart that pervades our entire body and extends beyond it. The piercing you feel may be shared by the nearest stone or a distant mountain. If it is so, this too is an arrow to your heart.

The voices in this book point to an almost forgotten knowledge: that humans belong on the earth, that the land celebrates us in our capacity to witness it and to feel it fully. The wild places awaken within us an innate untamed longing. This longing is itself a kind of wisdom. It guides us to awaken to who we are. Each step forward on this path is a right step, a holy step. The authors gathered here knew this intimately. Through their writing we can walk with them in a wild windswept landscape, their company that of teachers who knew how to hold the silence in which true companionship ripens.

Nowadays we can go into most natural areas with a relaxed and leisurely mind. We don't need to worry much about tigers or grizzly bears. Yet the wild places amplify even the smallest mistakes. Recently, while walking an easy trail in the New Mexico desert, a moment of inattention led to a misstep that has, at least for now, ruined my knee. The learning from this injury continues to unfold; our wounds also carry the voice of the wild. We are reminded to pay attention to the details, to not try to hurry things along. What is offered, what we need, will emerge on its own terms and in its own time, like ripening fruit. The journey is much more about being here than it is about getting there. For this we need a different kind of map. This book is one such map.

In these pages is the knowledge of the old Chinese master, transformed with time, like the weather and the forests, as the mountains themselves have changed. All along the volume I sought was in the library of wild places. In *Wild Wisdom*, the lost manuscript is returned to me and I am grateful.

—M. Amos Clifford, author of *Your Guide to Forest Bathing: Experience the Healing Power of Nature*

INTRODUCTION

Over centuries, explorers, mystics, and seekers from many traditions have sought inspiration in nature and solitude. Many of them not only spoke about the wilderness, described it, but also lived from it, bringing back to us a message in living, wild words.

This little book gathers sayings and stories from a selection of women and men who sank their roots so deeply into nature that the wisdom they created can still serve us today. Here you will find stories and sayings of the well-known Egyptian "desert fathers" (and the lesser known "desert mothers") as well as the voices of Russian forest hermits, Sufi mystics, Scottish mountain explorers, European novelists, wandering Chinese Taoists, Kashmiri hermits, Japanese Zen masters, American naturalists and scientists, and other generally rebellious eccentrics.

Many of them balanced time between solitude and society, challenging the status quo of their time. So the word *wild* here also means: unexpected, not obeying a pattern that their cultures took for granted. They found themselves as society's outliers, or even outlaws, by choice or constitution. For this reason, some needed to communicate indirectly—in meta-phor, poetry, or story.

Of course, many voices here rhapsodize about nature's beauty. But just as many celebrate the untamed, seeming chaos of nature, in which the edge between life and death is small and sharp. Wild nature's embrace of both the light and shadow of life also led many to feel that, just as humanity is embedded in nature, nature is embedded in a greater reality that is not merely beyond or above, but rather all around us and within us. They concluded that we are part of the wilderness (or wildness) we are looking for.

At heart, what unifies these voices is their insistence that one can bring inner nature and outer nature together. They weren't satisfied with simply thinking or emoting about nature. Instead, they dove into nature and attempted to dissolve the inner boundaries separating them from it. Then they decided what to do next in their lives. For some, this meant staying in the wilderness. For others, it meant returning to community and speaking directly from their experience.

As the Irish playwright Oscar Wilde says simply, returning to society after being jailed for homosexuality more than a hundred years ago:

> "It seems to me that we all look at nature too much, and live with her too little . . . . We call ours a utilitarian age, and we yet do not know the uses of any single thing. We have forgotten that water

can cleanse, and fire purify, and that the earth is mother to us all
. . . . Society, as we have constituted it, will have no place for me,
has none to offer. But nature, whose sweet rains fall on unjust and
just alike, will have clefts in the rocks where I may hide, and secret
valleys in whose silence I may weep undisturbed."

Instead of organizing the sayings, stories, musings, and poetry by philosophical, religious, or spiritual tradition, I have chosen to bring the speakers' voices together by the settings in which they found themselves: forests, mountains, deserts, rivers and ocean, and with nonhuman companions—fish, birds, animals, and insects, to name a few. One can see the effects of these different environments on the way our explorers express themselves.

To an overwhelming degree, we share the same bodies, the same ways of breathing and making sound, the same potentials for sensing nature. Each individual, of course, varies in subtle yet important ways. We differ first in our relationship to different environments and the unique ability we each possess to express this diversity. Of course, family upbringing and culture, including education, philosophy, and religion, immediately jump in between us and our direct experience; otherwise there would be too many impressions to take in at once. Yet family and culture also evolve over time from our collective relationship to *some* environment, actual or virtual. In this little book, I have chosen the voices and stories of those who, in one way or another, broke through these familial and cultural walls (or at least rattled them). This is why people remembered them.

Indeed, many recent voices are doing the same with increasing urgency, expressing what people have called eco-poetics, eco-spirituality, or eco-psychology. Our world's "house" or *oikos*, to use the Greek derivation of the word, does face grave threats. By choosing voices that are at least fifty years old, and some more than several thousand, I want to call our attention to a simple truth: we have a different heritage that can be followed—a lineage of ancestors worldwide who predate the increasingly virtual, homogenous, globalized consciousness that has overtaken us in the past few generations. Their prophetic words can presage a positive change in what has been the ever-changing story of human consciousness.

The first section, *Into the Wild Wood*, introduces us to a conversation between North American, Asian, Middle Eastern, and European voices. The dense, lush expression of their sayings, stories, and reports reflects the diversity of forest, woods, meadows, and marshes. It takes time to wend one's way through the woods. Paths don't proceed in straight, unimpeded lines, and often no paths exist. Here 19th-century American transcendentalists find themselves talking to 4th-century Taoists together with 7th-century Syrian mystics and 18th-century Hasidic storytellers.

Section two, *Taking a Mountain View*, brings us into the rarefied air and far-reaching views of mountains, hills, and valleys. Perspective is a unifying theme here. So are the awakened senses: taking care with each footstep and noticing the rocky, nearly impossible places in which life can choose to thrive. We also find here voices reflecting profound stillness and the experience of merging with the living rock of the mountain itself. As the early 20th-century German-Swiss novelist Hermann Hesse writes, while lying on a slope of the Alps:

> *And so for ten thousand years I lie there, and gaze into the heavens, and gaze into the lake. When I sneeze, there's a thunderstorm. When I breathe, the snow melts, and the waterfalls dance. When I die, the whole world dies. Then I journey across the world's ocean, to bring back a new sun.*

The mountains also evoke in some of our seekers unbridled ecstasy, as in the words of the 8th-century CE Chinese poet Bai Juyi:

> *I climb alone the path to the Eastern Rock.*
> *I lean my body on the banks of white stone, and*
> *with my hands I pull down a green cassia branch.*
> *My mad singing startles the valleys and hills.*

The third section, *Desert Sole*, takes us into the singular experience of being "alone with the alone"—those who sought, often in extreme ways, the experience of emptiness, inside and out. These explorers, hermits, and solitaries express the desert's uncompromising extremes, their words often stripped of grace and style, almost gnomic, like the desert after a sandstorm that brings sudden, irresistible change. As one of the secular voices, British military explorer T. E. Lawrence reflects:

> *Individual nomads had their revealed religion, not oral or traditional or expressed, but instinctive in themselves. And so we got all the Semitic creeds with, in character and essence, a stress on the emptiness of the world and the fullness of God. And they were expressed according to the power and opportunity of the believer.*

Section four, *The Magic of Water*, brings us into the presence of those who spent time in communion with streams, rivers, and oceans. Their love of water's fluid strength and constant variation balances their cautious awareness that the overwhelming power of water can bring death as well as life. As the early 20th-century French philosopher Simone Weil reflects succinctly:

> *The sea is no less beautiful to us because we know that sometimes boats sink. On the contrary, it is more beautiful.*

Others comment on the similarity between water and the way thoughts flow through our minds, as in the words of the 4th-century BCE Taoist Chuang Tzu:

When water is still, it is like a mirror, reflecting everything, your chin and eyebrows. And if water obtains lucidity from stillness, how much more will the faculties of the mind? The mind of the sage, being in repose, becomes the mirror of the universe, of all creation.

Section five introduces us to the *Wild Companions* that share the world with us. Our explorers reflect on everything from a flea to a fish, from bees and wild swans to dancing swifts. These voices express the uniqueness of the other living beings that surround us as well as our own impermanence. In the words of the Scottish-American naturalist John Muir from 1916:

This star, our own good earth, made many a successful journey around the heavens ere human beings were made, and whole realms of creatures enjoyed existence and returned to dust ere humans appeared to claim them.

After human beings have played their part in creation's plan, they may also disappear without any general burning or extraordinary commotion whatever.

Section six, *Speaking Wildly in Society* finds many of the same speakers returning from their explorations and, through word or action, delivering the messages they received from their time in nature. Some of them were received kindly in the corridors of power, many were not. Some offer critique, others display an "overcome by yielding" approach. Speaking to an audience in 1954, American scientist and naturalist Rachel Carson linked human treatment of nature with its spiritual life:

> *I believe that whenever we destroy beauty, or whenever we substitute something man-made and artificial for a natural feature of the earth, we have retarded some part of man's spiritual growth . . . . Our origins are of the earth. And so there is in us a deeply seated response to the natural universe, which is part of our humanity.*

Section seven, *Reading the Book of Nature*, could also be entitled "hearing the songs of nature." Sight, hearing, and all of the senses reveal to our seekers a larger vision of the life that humanity shares with nature. This chorus of voices from all parts of the earth expresses wonder, joy, awe, and fear in the face of the mysterious unity of human nature with its environment, as well as its collective unity within some larger, unnameable mystery. This rich, complex relationship seems to be a common human understanding that even those brought up in "modern" civilization rediscover. As the 19th-century American author Henry David Thoreau writes:

> *If I were to discover that a certain kind of stone by the pond-shore*
> *was affected, say partially disintegrated, by a particular natural*
> *sound, as of a bird or insect, I see that one could not be completely*
> *described without describing the other.*
>
> *I am that rock by the pond-side.*

Finally, the last section, *Wild to the End*, finds our community of
explorers reflecting on what nature tells them about death and
other possible journeys beyond our time-limited human life.
Some voices here have returned to solitude in nature after a
life of work in society. Others continue to look to the wild for
guidance up until the end, as in the words of the 14th-century
Kashmiri forest mystic Lalla:

> *One moment I saw a river flowing gently.*
> *The next, all bridges washed away.*
> *We are like snow falling in a river—*
> *a moment white, then melted forever.*

Selections you won't find here: indigenous voices from native
cultures around the world. First, whole books have been
rightly devoted to these voices from Africa, South and North
America, Australia, and Oceania. Seek them out. Those voices
express more whole, integrated views of nature than what are
prevalent in the so-called developed world today. The diversity of the indigenous languages, syntax, and grammar, often

including musical tone and nonverbal art, stands in stark contrast to the much more limited modern and postmodern ways of understanding life.

The voices I have collected here all come from North America, Europe, and Asia (including West Asia, aka the "Middle East"), areas that today contribute massively to our ecological problems but that can also contribute greatly to their possible solutions. Perhaps we can hear our own ancestors' voices as prophetic rather than merely exotic.

Some ancient stories and accounts of these pioneers come from hagiography, legend, or story. This includes those of the Egyptian desert fathers and mothers, as well as the Sufi mystic Rabia of Basra. However, this does not diminish the wisdom passed down by word of mouth, often authorless, rather than through written history. At the end of the book you will find an appendix that contains thumbnail sketches of each of the voices as well as a bibliography for further exploration. Where possible, I have given exact dates for each selection, but sometimes only an approximate century is possible.

What you also won't find here: more. It's a little book, by definition and by design. It's designed that way to perhaps substitute (in size) for the digital device to which you'd like to give a rest. For an hour, or a day?

Also not to be found: agreement. Some selections may elicit a nod, others a vigorous shake, still others a scratch of the head. Maybe those that raise disagreement, or more questions, can kick-start your own process of finding the harmony between chaos and order that wild nature represents.

No doubt readers will have their own favorites. This is a personal, rather than any sort of representative selection (what would be representative of nature's extreme diversity, I wonder?). Some voices reappear, others are heard only once. Rather than sending me your favorites, why not compile your own anthology of ancestors who inspire you? Then travel with them into nature, take some time to breathe and just be, and write down (or draw or sing or dance) your own reflections.

• • •

Heading into the hills above our Scottish home, at the entrance to the nature district, I recently passed a van owned by the local woodland trust. Stenciled on the side of the van in large, block letters was the simple message "WE ALL NEED TREES."

Given that this particular nature district is a "mixed use area," including farmland for grazing and planting as well as open-space forest, meadow, hills, streams, burns, and reservoirs, it occurred to me that different people would hear the word *need* differently. Need for raw materials, need for food, need to absorb carbon dioxide from the atmosphere, need for clean air and water, or need for inspiration. I suppose that the simple phrase "We all . . . " covers it well enough to elicit an inner "yes" from whoever sees the van.

With all the valid, pressing concerns about the environment today, one area we usually overlook is the role that nature plays in the ways we actually think and feel. The latest research about our genetic inheritance reveals that the genes in the human body do not encode our future health to any exactitude. They act only as a blueprint or an outline. Our environment interacts with our genes, causing them to turn on and off at various times and to express themselves differently in different people. The field of research is now called *epigenetics*. This is why uncovering the "secrets of the human genome," a project so touted twenty years ago as the cure to all disease, didn't quite pan out as envisioned.

It may be obvious that a child raised in an intensely urban environment, who seldom sees or touches trees or grass, will grow and develop differently from one raised in the country. It turns out, however, that all our nervous systems are biologically wrapped around and interwoven with our environment. Critical damage to this environment impairs humanity's actual ability to think and feel clearly and to envision a positive, healthy future for itself.

Which brings us back to ourselves. Retreating in nature, working in the garden, even sitting on a park bench for a few minutes, can refresh and balance lives mostly surrounded by the products of human culture. Hopefully, hearing the voices of some of these early natural explorers can whet our appetite for our own wildness. It might also help us remember not only what the natural world offers us physically, but also what it inspires as food for our inner lives.

—Neil Douglas-Klotz,
Lomond Hills, Fife, Scotland

WILD
WISDOM

1

Into
the Wild
Wood

I Went to the Woods

I went to the woods, because I wished to live deliberately, to face only the essential facts of life and to see if I could not learn what it had to teach.

I did not want, when I came to die, to discover that I had not lived.

I wanted to live deep and suck out all the marrow of life, to live so sturdily and spartan-like as to put to rout all that was not life. To cut a broad swath and shave close, to drive life into a corner and reduce it to its lowest terms.

If life proved to be mean—why then to get the whole and genuine meanness of it and publish its meanness to the world. Or if it were sublime, to know it by experience and be able to give a true account of it in my next excursion.

Most people, it appears to me, are in a strange uncertainty about it—whether life is of the devil or of God—and have somewhat hastily concluded that it is the chief end of people to "glorify God and enjoy him forever."

—Henry David Thoreau, 1854 (*Walden*), USA.

A Tree of No Use

Hui Tzu said to Chuang Tzu, "I have a large tree that people call the ailanthus. Its trunk swells out to a large size, but the carpenter's tools cannot be used on it, because its branches are knotted and crooked. So although it grows everywhere, builders do not even turn their heads to look at it.

"It's just like with your words, Chuang Tzu," he continued. "They are great, but of no use. Everyone agrees in ignoring them."

Chuang Tzu replied, "Have you never seen a wildcat or a weasel? It just lies there, crouching and low, until a hunter approaches. Then it jumps all around, east and west, high and low, until it is caught in a trap, or dies in a net.

"Or take the yak. It's so large, it is like a cloud hanging in the sky. It's really large, but it cannot catch mice.

"So you have a large tree and are bothered because it is of no use. Why don't you plant it in land where there is nothing else, or in a wide and barren wilderness? There you might saunter idly by it, or enjoy untroubled, easy sleep beneath it.

"Neither hook nor axe would shorten its existence. There would be nothing to injure it. So by virtue of being useless, it succeeds in completing its allotted life span.

"What is there in its uselessness to distress you?"

—Inner Books of Chuang Tzu,
4th century BCE, China.

The Preaching of Trees

For me, trees have always been the most penetrating preachers. I revere them when they live in tribes and families, in forests and groves. And even more I revere them when they stand alone.

In their highest boughs the world rustles, their roots rest in infinity. But they do not lose themselves there; they struggle with all the force of their lives for one thing only: to fulfill themselves according to their own laws, to build up their own form, to represent themselves.

Trees are sanctuaries. Whoever knows how to speak to them, whoever knows how to listen to them, can learn the truth. They do not preach learning and precepts. They preach, undeterred by particulars, the ancient law of life.

A tree says: A kernel is hidden in me, a spark, a thought. I am life from eternal life. The attempt and the risk that the eternal mother took with me are unique, unique the form and veins of my skin, unique the smallest play of leaves in my branches and the smallest scar on my bark. I was made to form and reveal the eternal in my own smallest special detail.

A tree says: My strength is trust. I know nothing about my father. I know nothing about the thousand children that every year spring out of me. I live out the secret of my seed to the very end and care for nothing else. I trust that God is in me. I trust that my labor is holy. Out of this trust I live.

When we are stricken and cannot bear our lives any longer, then a tree has something to say to us: Be still! Be still! Look at me! Life is not easy, life is not difficult. Those are childish thoughts. Let God speak within you, and your thoughts will grow silent. You are anxious because your path leads away from mother and home. But every step and every day lead you back again to the mother. Home is neither here nor there. Home is within you, or home is nowhere at all.

A longing to wander tears my heart when I hear trees rustling in the wind at evening. If one listens to them silently for a long time, this longing reveals its kernel, its meaning. It is not so much a matter of escaping from one's suffering, though it may seem to be so. It is a longing for home, for a memory of the mother, for new metaphors for life. It leads home. Every path leads homeward, every step is birth, every step is death, every grave is mother.

So the tree rustles in the evening, when we stand uneasy before our childish thoughts. Trees have long thoughts, long breathing and restful, just as they have longer lives than ours. They are wiser than we are, as long as we do not listen to them. But when we have learned how to listen to trees, then the brevity and the quickness and the childlike hastiness of our thoughts achieve an incomparable joy. Those who have learned to listen to trees no longer want to be a tree. They want to be nothing except what they are. That is home. That is happiness.

—Hermann Hesse, 1917–1918
(*Wandering*), Germany-Switzerland.

My Branches Weigh Me Down

Say what you will, and scratch my heart to find
the roots of last year's roses in my breast.
I am as surely riper in my mind,
as if the fruit stood in the stalls confessed.
Laugh at the unshed leaf, say what you will,
call me in all things what I was before,
a flutterer in the wind, a woman still.
I tell you I am what I was and more.
My branches weigh me down, frost cleans the air,
my sky is black with small birds bearing south.
Say what you will, confuse me with fine care,
put aside my word as but an April truth.
Autumn is no less on me, that a rose
hugs the brown bough and sighs before it goes.

—Edna St. Vincent Millay, 1922, USA.

Discarding Old Leaves

A tree will not produce new buds until it has let go of its old leaves. So solitary seekers will not produce new buds until they shake the memory of their past from their hearts.

The wind makes the fruits ripe, just as the breath of the Holy One ripens the soul's fruits.

Unripe fruits taste sour and disagreeable. People can't eat them until the sun sweetens them. So a solitary seeker's first efforts at letting go taste bitter and very unpleasant and don't offer any comfort. Later, contemplation sweetens the heart as it withdraws from everything unnecessary and superficial. Then the heart can forget its own self.

—Isaac of Nineveh, 7th century CE, Eastern Arabia.

The Freest Tree

Someone asked a wise person, "Of the many celebrated trees that Allah has created, some are very lofty, some wonderfully shady or fruit-giving. But people call none of them *azad* or free, except for the cypress, which is none of these. Can you explain this mystery?"

That wise one replied, "Trees produce fruit or shade only during their appointed seasons. Sometimes they are fresh and blooming, other times dry and withered. The cypress isn't exposed to either condition: it always flourishes. The azads, the spiritually independent ones, share the same quality. They don't depend on the time or season for their freshness."

Don't set your heart on what passes away. The Tigris will continue to flow through Baghdad after the run of the Khalifs is extinct.

If your hand has plenty, be liberal and give freely like the date tree.

But you have nothing to give away, be an azad, a free person, like the cypress.

—Saadi Shirazi, 13th century CE
(*The Rose Garden*), Persia (now Iran).

The Tree of Our Original Nature

In one way, our original nature has no desires, but in another way, I can say original nature is all desire at once. When it flows out like water, like air, it flows out infinitely, but it is limited.

It will take the beautiful shape of a tree, according to time and space. The desire to flow out from the seed will create the beautiful crystallizations of branches, leaves, and flowers. That is the symbol of our desires.

When we look at our desires from the outside, we see them whole, like the growth of a tree. But when we see them from the inside, we see joy, hatred, agony, love. It is a natural phenomenon that we experience every day.

But sometimes we look at it from the outside.

It is a forest, a complete design.

—Sokei-an Sasaki, 1935–39 (*Original Nature*),
Japan-USA.

Song of the Traveling Trees

A few minutes ago every tree was excited, bowing to the roaring storm—waving, swirling, tossing their branches in glorious enthusiasm, like worship.

But though to the outer ear these trees are now silent, their songs never cease. Every hidden cell is throbbing with music and life, every fiber thrilling like harp strings, while incense is ever flowing from the balsam bells and leaves.

No wonder the hills and groves were God's first temples, and the more they are cut down and hewn into cathedrals and churches, the farther off and dimmer seems the Lord himself.

We all travel the Milky Way together, trees and people. But it never occurred to me until this stormy day, while swinging in the wind, that trees are travelers.

They make many journeys, not very extensive ones, it is true, but our own little comings and goings are only little more than tree-wavings.

Many of them not so much.

—John Muir, 1869 (*My First Summer in the Sierra*), 1894 (*The Mountains of California*), Scotland-USA.

Mulberry and Bamboo Groves Neglected

I always loved to walk the woods and mountains.
Pleased myself, lost in fields and marshes.
Now I go out with nephews and nieces
in the wilds, parting hazel branches,
back and forth through the mounds and hollows.
All around us lie signs of ancient peoples,
remnants of their broken hearths and wells.
Mulberry and bamboo groves neglected.
Stop and ask the simple woodsman,
"Where have all these people gone now?"
Turning he looks quietly and tells me,
"Nothing's left of them, they're finished."
One world. Though the lives we lead are different,
in courts of power or labouring in the market,
these are more than empty words:
Our life's a play of light and shade,
returning at last to the void.

—Tao Yuanming, 4th–5th century CE, China.

Swamp Thoughts

Would it not be a luxury to stand up to one's chin in some retired swamp for a whole summer's day, scenting the sweet fern and bilberry blows, and lulled by the minstrelsy of gnats and mosquitoes?

Say . . . twelve hours of genial and familiar conversation with the leopard frog? The sun to rise from behind alder and dogwood, and then climb buoyantly to the meridian of three hands' breadth, and finally sink to rest behind some bold western hummock.

To hear the evening chant of the mosquito from a thousand green chapels and the bittern begin to boom from its concealed fort like a sunset gun!

Surely one may as profitably be soaked in the juices of a marsh for one day as pick one's way dry-shod over sand.

Cold and damp—are they not as rich experiences as warmth and dryness? So is not shade as good as sunshine, night as day?

Why be eagles and thrushes always, and owls and whip-poor-wills never?

—Henry David Thoreau, 1840 (Journals), USA.

Long Barefoot Walks

Ah, how I believe in it, in life.

Not the life constituted by time but this other life, the life of small things, the life of animals and of the great plains. This life that continues through millennia with no apparent investment in anything, and yet with all of its forces of movement and growth and warmth in complete harmony.

This is why cities weigh on me so heavily. This is why I love taking long barefoot walks where I will not miss a grain of sand and will make available to my body the entire world in many shapes, as sensation, as experience, as something to relate to.

This is why I exist wherever possible on vegetables alone, in order to come close to a simple awareness of life unaided by anything alien. That is why I will not drink wine, because I want nothing but my juices to speak out and rush through me and attain bliss, the way they do in children and animals, from deep within the self!

And this is also why I want to strip myself of all arrogance and not consider myself superior to the tiniest animal or any more wonderful than a stone. But to be what I am, to live what I was meant to live, to want to sound like no one else, to yield the blossoms dictated to my heart: this is what I want—and this surely cannot be arrogance.

—Rainer Maria Rilke, 1903, Austria-Bohemia
(now Czech Republic).

The Grass Does Not Refuse

The grass does not refuse to
flourish in the spring wind.
The leaves are not angry at
falling through the autumn sky.
Who, with whip or spur,
can quicken the feet of time?
The things of the world
flourish and decay,
each at their own hour.

—Li Bai, 8th century CE, China.

The Job Description of Grass

The grass so little has to do—
a sphere of simple green
with only butterflies to brood
and bees to entertain
and stir all day to pretty tunes,
the breezes fetch along.
And hold the sunshine in its lap
and bow to everything.
And thread the dews all night,
like pearls, and make itself so fine—
a duchess were too common
for such a noticing.
And even when it dies, to pass
in odors so divine,
as lowly spices gone to sleep
or amulets of pine.
And then to dwell in sovereign barns
and dream the days away.
The grass so little has to do,
I wish I were the hay!

—Emily Dickinson, 1830–1886, USA.

Songs of the Plants

When one becomes worthy to hear the songs of plants, how each plant speaks its song to God, how beautiful and sweet it is to hear the singing!

It is good indeed to serve God in the middle of them all, wandering alone over the fields between growing things.

All the speech of the fields then enters into your own and intensifies its strength.

With every breath you drink in the air of paradise, and when you return home the world is renewed in your eyes.

—Rabbi Nachman of Bratslav, 18th century,
Russia-Ukraine.

Sunflower

Everybody knows the sunflower plant. It always turns its yellow head to the sun, reaching out to it. That's where it got its name. But if the sunflower stops turning to the sun, then gardeners say that it has begun to deteriorate, it has got a worm, it should be cut off.

Likewise the soul longs to orient itself to the divine, it lines itself up in the right direction, and stretches to the source of light like the sunflower. But if it stops doing this, that soul is on the way to death.

—Father Varsonofy of Optina, 19th century, Russia.

Life Is in the Forests

In the forests, there is no justice.
No, and no punishment there,
and if the willow casts its shadow on the earth,
the cypress will not say,
"This is heresy against the Book."
The justice of the people is snow.
If seen by the sun, it would melt.

Give me the nay and sing,
for singing is the justice of hearts,
and the moan of the nay endures
after sins perish.

In the forests, I have found no difference
between the self and the body.
Wind is water tossed,
and dew is water stilled,
and fragrance is flowers swaying,
and soil is flowers stilled,
and the shadows of the poplar are nymphs
who thought it was night and went to sleep.

Give me the nay and sing,
for singing is the body and soul,
and the moan of the nay endures
beyond what is drunk
in the morning or evening.

Nothing is barren in the forests.
No, and there is no alien there.
Within the dates is a kernel that
preserves the secret of the palms,
and within the honeycomb is a token
of the fields and of the hive.
What is *barren* but a term composed
of the essence of idleness.

Give me the nay and sing,
for singing is a body that flows,
and the moan of the nay endures
beyond the misshapen and ill-begotten.

Life is in the forests,
and if the days were in my hands,
they would be scattered in the forests.
But Time has a purpose in my self.
Whenever I seek a forest, he apologizes.

And there are pathways of destiny
that will not be changed,
for which people fall short of
reaching their goals.

—Kahlil Gibran, 1918 (*The Processions*),
USA and Syria/Lebanon.

2

Taking
a Mountain
View

You Ask Me Why

You ask me why I live in the
blue jade mountains.
My heart is at leisure with itself.
I smile and do not answer.
The peach blossom floats away
on flowing water.
Here is neither heaven nor earth,
timeless, space-less,
even for a human being.

—Li Bai, 8th century CE, China.

Mind Stretching

After looking at the Alps,
I felt that my mind had been stretched
beyond the limits of its elasticity
and fitted so loosely on
my old ideas of space that
I had to spread these to fit it.

—Oliver Wendell Holmes, 1858
(*The Autocrat of the Breakfast Table*), USA.

Mountains and Seas

Perhaps it is not strange that I, who greatly love the sea, should find much in the mountains to remind me of it. I cannot watch the headlong descent of the hill streams without remembering that, though their journey be long, its end is in the sea. And always in these Appalachian highlands there are reminders of those ancient seas that more than once lay over all this land.

Halfway up the steep path to the lookout is a cliff formed of sandstone. Long ago it was laid down under shallow marine waters where strange and unfamiliar fishes swam. Then the seas receded, the mountains were uplifted, and now wind and rain are crumbling the cliff away to the sandy particles that first composed it. And these whitened limestone rocks on which I am sitting—these too were formed under that Paleozoic ocean of the myriad tiny skeletons of creatures that drifted in its water.

Now I lie back with half closed eyes and try to realize that I am at the bottom of another ocean—an ocean of air on which the hawks are sailing.

> —Rachel Carson, 1945 (Field Notes at Hawk
> Mountain Sanctuary, Pennsylvania), USA.

Becoming an Alp

I stretch out my legs in the grass, and I wish they could be longer. I wish I could be a giant, then I could lie with my head near the snows on one of the Alps, lie there among the goats, with my toes splashing below in the deep lake.

So I would lie there and never get up again, between my fingers the bushes would grow, and the wild roses of the Alps in my hair, my knees would be alpine foothills, and vineyards would stand on my body, and houses, and chapels.

And so for ten thousand years I lie there, and gaze into the heavens and gaze into the lake. When I sneeze, there's a thunderstorm. When I breathe, the snow melts, and the waterfalls dance. When I die, the whole world dies. Then I journey across the world's ocean, to bring back a new sun.

Where am I going to sleep tonight? Who cares! What is the world doing? Have new gods been discovered, new laws, new freedoms? Who cares!

But up here a primrose is blossoming and bearing silver fuzz on its leaves, and the light sweet wind is singing below me in the poplars, and between my eyes and heaven a dark golden bee is hovering and humming—I care about that. It is humming the song of happiness, humming the song of eternity. Its song is my history of the world.

—Hermann Hesse, 1917–18 (*Wandering*),
Germany-Switzerland.

Sleeping with the Mountain

Well, I have discovered my mountain—its weathers, its airs and lights, its singing burns, its haunted dells, its pinnacles and tarns, its birds and flowers, its snows, its long blue distances. Year by year, I have grown in familiarity with them all.

But if the whole truth of them is to be told as I have found it, I too am involved. I have been the instrument of my own discovering; and to govern the stops of the instrument needs learning too. Thus the senses must be trained and disciplined, the eye to look, the ear to listen, the body must be trained to move with the right harmonies. I can teach my body many skills by which to learn the nature of the mountain. One of the most compelling is quiescence.

A 4 a.m. start leaves plenty of time for these hours of quiescence, and perhaps of sleep, on the summits. One's body is limber with the sustained rhythm of mounting, and relaxed in the ease that follows the eating of food. One is as tranquil as the stones, rooted far down in their immobility. The soil is no more a part of the earth. If sleep comes at such a moment, its coming is a movement as natural as day. And after—ceasing to be a stone, to be the soil of the earth, opening eyes that have human cognisance behind them upon what one has been so profoundly a part of. That is all.

One has been in.

—Nan Shepherd, 1947
(*The Living Mountain*), Scotland.

Offspring of Mountains

The horizon has one kind of beauty and attraction for one who has never explored the hills and mountains, and another—I fear a less ethereal and glorious one—to the one who has.

That blue mountain on the horizon, which we have not climbed, on which we have not camped for a night, is certainly the most heavenly, the most elysian.

But it's only that our horizon is moved thus further off. If, for instance, our whole life so far has proven a failure, then the future that can atone for everything, where there must still be some success, will be even more glorious.

In every country the mountains are fountains, not only of rivers but of people. Therefore we all are born mountaineers, the offspring of rock and sunshine.

Thousands of tired, nerve-shaken, over-civilized people are beginning to find out that going to the mountains is going home. That wildness is a necessity, and that mountain parks and reservations are useful not only as fountains of timber and irrigating rivers but as fountains of life.

—John Muir, 1851, 1875 (letters to editor), 1901
(*Our National Parks*), Scotland-USA.

Climbing to the Top

Up and up, the Incense-burner Peak!
My heart stores what my eyes and ears perceive.
All the year detained by official business,
today at last I got a chance to go.
Grasping the creepers, I cling to dangerous rocks.
My hands and feet, weary with groping for a hold.
There came with me three or four friends,
but two friends dared not go further.
At last we reach the topmost crest of the peak.
My eyes are blinded, my soul rocks and reels.
The chasm beneath me—ten thousand feet.
The ground I stand on, only a foot wide.
If you have not exhausted
your ability to see and hear,
how can you realize the
wideness of the world?
The waters of the river look as narrow as a ribbon,
P'en Castle smaller than one's fist.
How it clings, the dust of the world's halter!
It chokes my limbs, I cannot shake it away.
Thinking of retirement from public life,
I heave an envious sigh and then, with lowered head,
I come back to the ants' nest.

—Bai Juyi, 8th–9th century CE, China.

Like the White Lion

Like the white lion living on the mountain
you should not go to the valley,
otherwise your nice mane will become dirty.
To keep it in good order you should
remain in the snowy hill, as you could.
Like the great eagle flying above the mountain—
it never falls into a hole—
your wings would break completely.
To keep them in good order you should
remain in the snowy mountain, as you could.
Like the tigress that passes by the mountain
and stays only in the deep forest—
on the plain you'd have no rest.
To keep in good order you should
remain in the snowy hill, as you could.
Like the golden-eyed fish
that swims only in the central sea
so that the fisher doesn't see it—
to keep in good order you should
remain in the snowy hill, as you could.

—Milarepa, 9th–10th century CE, Tibet.

A Timeless Hollow

High rises the eastern peak
soaring up into the blue sky.
Among the rocks, an empty hollow—
secret, still, mysterious!
Uncarved and unhewn,
screened by nature
with a roof of clouds.
Time and the seasons—
what things do you bring to my life
with your ceaseless change?
I will live forever in this hollow
where springs and autumns
pass unnoticed.

—Hsieh Tao-yün, 4th century CE, China.

Spirit of the Valley

The spirit of the valley never dies,
the mystic mother whose pregnant womb
gives birth to all things.
That's why she is called
the root of nature.
Simply hold onto this, and
you will not need to work to understand.

—Lao Tze, 6th century BCE
(from the Tao Te Ching), China.

The Valley of Knowing and Not-Knowing

When you enter this valley, realize that it has no beginning or end. No other road is like the hidden road there, and one person's road is not the same as another's.

Everyone finds a path revealed according to their capacity, and everyone's progress depends on their state of breath. How could it be otherwise?

Even if a gnat could fly with all its strength, it couldn't outrace the wind. No two birds fly alike, each finds its own route.

So some go by way of the mosque's niche. Others by way of idols.

When the sun of knowing shines, everyone receives the light according to their ability. And when that sun shines, the world's rubbish bin turns into a rose garden. The rind reveals its kernel.

The lover no longer sees any particle of self, only the Beloved.

Wherever one looks, one sees the face of the One, and every atom of life reveals Reality's presence.

—Fariduddin Attar, 13th century CE
(*The Conference of the Birds*), Persia (now Iran).

Those Who Sit on the Mountain

Nature is united with divine love, to which the will of the soul is also joined. Nature is well ordered and asks nothing that is against the laws of the divine.

Love says to us, "There are those who sit on the mountain above the winds and rain. They are not ashamed of anything in the earth or nature, nor do they fear anything that might happen.

"These people are real people—with faith, their doors open, not grieving. Nor do any of their works of service come to nothing. They are the ones who sit on the mountain, none other."

—Marguerite Porete, 13th century
(*The Mirror of Simple Souls*), France.

The Zen of Mountains

When I came to this country and was tramping through the Cascade Mountains, the mountains following the Columbia River, I felt that the soil of America had the essence of Zen.

The nature of the American people is like those cedar trees in the Cascade Mountains, rather coarse-grained but straight and simple.

Zen is inborn in Americans. They have this precious jewel in their minds. It was given to them by nature, but this has not yet been disclosed. So they have never discovered this jewel in their nature.

Hereafter, perhaps in three hundred years, someone will come and open the box for you, and you will find the jewel for yourselves.

—Sokei-an Sasaki, 1935–39 (Lectures), Japan, USA.

Using a Telescope

Many people, when I tell them that I have been on a mountain, ask if I took a telescope with me.

No doubt I could have seen further with such a glass and seen particular objects more distinctly. I could have counted more meeting houses, but this has nothing to do with the peculiar beauty and grandeur of the view that an elevated position affords.

It was not to see a few particular objects, as if they were near at hand, as I had been accustomed to see them, that I ascended the mountain. It was to see an infinite variety, far and near, in their relation to each other, reduced to a single picture.

In comparison with poetry, the facts of science tend to be as vulgar, like looking from the mountain with a telescope. It is just counting meeting houses.

—Henry David Thoreau, 1852 (Journals), USA.

Walk Away Quietly

Walk away quietly in any direction and taste the freedom of the mountaineer. Camp out among the grass and gentians of glacier meadows, in craggy garden nooks full of nature's darlings. Climb the mountains and get their good tidings.

Nature's peace will flow into you as sunshine flows into trees. The winds will blow their own freshness into you, and the storms their energy, while cares will drop off like autumn leaves.

As age comes on, one source of enjoyment after another is closed, but nature's sources never fail.

The petty discomforts that beset the awkward guest, the unskilled camper, are quickly forgotten, while all that is precious remains. Fears vanish as soon as one is fairly free in the wilderness.

Accidents in the mountains are less common than in the lowlands. And these mountain mansions are decent, delightful—even divine—places to die in, compared with the doleful chambers of civilization.

Few places in this world are more dangerous than home. Fear not, therefore, to try the mountain passes. They will kill care, save you from deadly apathy, set you free, and call forth every faculty into vigorous, enthusiastic action.

Even the sick should try these so-called dangerous passes, because for every unfortunate they kill, they cure a thousand.

—John Muir, 1898 (*Atlantic Magazine*), 1894
(*The Mountains of California*), Scotland-USA.

Madly Singing in the Mountains

There is no one among us that has not a special failing,
and my failing consists in writing verses.
I have broken away from the thousand ties of life,
but this infirmity still remains behind.
Each time that I look at a fine landscape,
each time that I meet a loved friend,
I raise my voice and recite a stanza of poetry
and am as glad as if a god had crossed my path.
Ever since the day I was banished to Hsiin-yang,
half my time I have lived among the hills.
And often, when I have finished a new poem,
I climb alone the path to the Eastern Rock.
I lean my body on the banks of white stone, and
with my hands I pull down a green cassia branch.
My mad singing startles the valleys and hills.
The apes and birds all come to look.
Fearing to become a laughingstock to the world,
I choose a place where no one goes.

—Bai Juyi, 8th–9th century CE, China.

3

Desert
Sole

To Wake in the Desert

To wake in that desert dawn was like waking in the heart of an opal.

The mists lifting their heads out of the hollows, the dews floating in ghostly wreaths from the black tents—both were shot through first with the faint glories of the eastern sky and then with the strong yellow rays of the risen sun.

The glorious cold air intoxicated every sense and set the blood throbbing.

To my mind the saying about the Bay of Naples should run differently: "See the desert on a fine morning, and die—if you can."

—Gertrude Bell, 1907 (*The Desert and the Sown: Travels in Palestine and Syria*), England.

Awake in the Desert Night

Once we had marched all night long with a caravan and halted toward morning on the outskirts of a desert wilderness. One of the company, who was clearly distracted, started wailing and yelling at dawn and then went wandering off into the desert. He didn't stop yelling for a moment.

When he returned to camp the next day, I asked him, "What was your problem, some mental condition or other?"

He replied, "No! I noticed the nightingales had come to sing in the groves, the pheasants to chatter together on the mountains, the frogs to croak in the pools, and the wild beasts to roar in the forests. Then I thought, 'It can't be right that all of nature is awake to praise Allah, and I am wrapt up in the sleep of forgetfulness!'

"So it was that first bird singing that set me off. It stole my patience and reason, my courage and understanding.

"My first wail reached the ear of a dear friend sleeping near me. He exclaimed, 'I can't believe a bird singing can upset a person like this!'

"I replied, 'But it also can't be proper conduct for a human being—all the birds singing the praise of Unity, and I am silent!'"

—Saadi Shirazi, 13th century CE (*The Rose Garden*),
Persia (now Iran).

The Creed of the Desert

This creed of the desert seemed inexpressible in words and indeed in thought. It was easily felt as an influence, and those who went into the desert long enough to forget its open spaces and its emptiness were inevitably thrust upon God as the only refuge and rhythm of being.

Individual nomads had their revealed religion, not oral or traditional or expressed, but instinctive in themselves. And so we got all the Semitic creeds with, in character and essence, a stress on the emptiness of the world and the fullness of God. And those creeds were expressed according to the power and opportunity of the believer.

—T. E. Lawrence, 1922 (*Seven Pillars of Wisdom*), England (in Arabia).

Desert Love: No Compromise

Once when Rabia al-Adawiyya was travelling on a pilgrimage to Mecca, she found herself alone in the desert for several days.

All of a sudden she saw the black outline of the Kaaba, the large rectangular building at the center of the pilgrim's devotion in Mecca, travelling toward her.

"Go back!" she cried out to the Kaaba. "What do I want with you? Your power and beauty mean nothing to me. I need the owner of the house to welcome me, the One who said, 'Whoever comes nearer to me by a hand's breadth, I will approach by the length of an arm.'"

Another time, she heard a voice saying: "Hey, holy woman, do you love the presence of the divine glory?"

"I do."

"And so do you hate Satan?"

"Because I love the ultimate Source of compassion," she replied, "I am unable to hate Satan. Once I saw the Prophet Muhammad in a dream. He asked me, 'Rabia, do you love me?' I replied, 'O Prophet, who doesn't love you? But love of Allah has filled my heart, so there is no place for either loving or hating anyone else.'"

—Stories tol told by Fariduddin Attar,
12th century, Persia, about the desert saint
Rabia al-Adawiyya, 8th century, Iraq.

Ruined House

It is dangerous for anyone to teach spiritual matters who has not first been trained in the practical life.

If someone who owns a ruined house receives guests there, that person may do the visitors harm, because of the run-down condition of the dwelling.

It's the same in the case of someone who has not first built an interior dwelling, connecting their inner and outer life. That person causes loss to those who come.

By words you might convert them to the right way, but by unripe behavior, you injure them.

Likewise, just as it's impossible to be both a plant and a seed at the same moment, so it's impossible to be surrounded by worldly honor and at the same time bear heavenly fruit.

—Amma Syncletica, 4th century CE, Egypt.

Rising and Falling

One of the Egyptian desert monks asked Father Sisoes,

"Abba, I have fallen. What should I do?"

"Get up again!" he replied.

"But I have fallen and risen again many times. How long do I need to go on?"

Father Sisoes replied, "Until death overtakes you in one of them—either rising up or falling down!"

—Story of Abba Sisoes of Scete,
5th century CE, Egypt.

Death before My Eyes

"Let me tell you what our life in the desert is like," said Amma Sara to someone who wanted to join her.

"I put out my foot to go up a ladder, then I place death before my eyes before beginning to climb."

—Saying of Amma Sara,
5th century CE, Egypt.

Visiting the Graveyard

One day a brother came to Abba Macarius the Egyptian and asked him, "Father, can you please give me some advice, so that I might live according to your way?"

Abba Macarius replied, "All right. Go to the cemetery and begin to verbally insult the dead. Come back when you've done so."

The brother went and abused those in their graves and even began to stone them. He returned and reported to Abba Macarius.

The old man asked him, "Didn't they say anything to you?"

The brother looked at him strangely and replied, "No."

"All right," said Abba Macarius, "then tomorrow go and praise them. Call them apostles, saints, and great righteous souls."

The next day the brother returned and said, "So, now I have praised them."

The old man asked, "And did they answer you?"

"No, of course not!"

"So you see," said the Abba. "You insulted them, and they said nothing to you. You praised them, and they did the same. If you are going to follow our way, follow their example. If you want to live, become dead, so that you don't care about either people's praise or blame.

"The dead care for nothing. In the same way you will learn to live."

—Story of Abba Macarius of Egypt, 4th century
CE, Egypt.

You Were Iron

Suffering?
So you were iron,
but fire has burnt the rust off you.
Falling ill?
If you stay in touch with your soul,
you will go from strength to strength.
Did you think you're already gold?
Then you will surely pass
through fire and be purged.

—Amma Syncletica of Alexandria,
4th century CE, Egypt.

Starting a Quarrel in the Desert

Once there were two old desert fathers who lived together for many years and never quarreled.

One day one said to the other, "Come on, let's pick a fight with each other, just as other people do. We need to know what it's like."

His companion answered, "But I don't know how a quarrel starts."

The first old man said, "Look, it's like this. I will set a brick between us and say, 'This is mine!' And then you say something like, 'Rubbish! It's not yours, it's mine!' And then the fight begins. Understand?"

So they placed a brick between them, and the first brother said, "This is mine!"

His companion yelled, "But that's not so, it's mine!"

Then immediately the first replied and said, "Oh, all right. Don't get so upset. It the brick is yours, just take it and go."

So they were unable to start a quarrel.

—Story of the desert fathers, 4th–5th centuries CE,
Egypt, from Palladius Hieronymus,
4th–5th centuries CE (*The Book of Paradise*)

Driving in the Gobi Desert

When you drive your automobile in the Gobi desert, you can go everywhere. There is no one-way road.

So the nature of your mind pervades in all directions at once, evenly, as light or heat penetrates evenly.

The original nature of human beings is this even nature, but we are now in uneven nature, and our automobile must be driven on a one-way road. We cannot spread ourselves evenly in all directions like radio waves.

We must move in one long line, like a telegraph line.

—Sokei-an Sasaki, 1935–39 (Lectures), Japan-USA.

How to Lose the Way

Once when Abba John and the brothers who accompanied him were traveling from Scete to another desert monastery, the young brother who was guiding them became confused and lost the way. Night was falling and they didn't know where they were, but the brother led on.

The other brothers whispered to Abba John, "Father, what will we do? This brother has lost the way, and—God forbid—we could all die wandering around in the desert at night!"

Abba John replied, "If you say anything to our guide he will feel guilty and ashamed. Look, I will pretend to be sick and will say that I am not able to go on any further."

"Good idea," replied the other brothers, and that's what they did. They stayed where they were until the morning rather than reproach the brother who was guiding them. Then by the sun the way was clear again.

> —Story of the desert fathers, 4th–5th centuries,
> Egypt, from Palladius Hieronymus,
> 4th–5th centuries CE (*The Book of Paradise*).

Falling Asleep

Once some of the old men went to Abba Poemen for advice and asked, "If we see our brothers sleeping during communal prayers, should we hit them to wake them up?"

The Abba replied, "If I see my brother sleeping, I place his head on my lap and give him a place to rest."

One of the other old men then asked him, "And so what do you say to God about this behavior?"

Abba Poemen replied, "I say to God, 'you have said, "First take the plank out of your own eye, and then you will be able to see to take the speck of dust out of the eye of your brother."'"

> —Story of the desert fathers, 4th–5th centuries,
> Egypt, from Palladius Hieronymus,
> 4th–5th centuries CE (*The Book of Paradise*).

Food in the Desert

Once a certain monk left his worldly occupations and lived in a small monastic community in the Egyptian desert for a number of years. He was humble and gracious to everyone. All the brothers wondered at the way he easily gave up meat then went into the desert alone and lived there for several years, eating only wild herbs.

After returning to the community, he prayed to God to tell him what reward he might have for all this abstinence. An angel was sent to say to him, "Leave this desert and travel along the road. You will see a certain shepherd of such-and-such an appearance who will greet you. According to what he tells you, you will receive."

The monk did all this and met the shepherd described by the angel. The shepherd greeted him, and having sat down to talk with each other, the monk saw in the shepherd's bag some green herbs he didn't recognize. He asked him, "What is this herb?"

The shepherd replied, "It's my food." And the monk asked him, "How long have you been feeding yourself on these green herbs?"

The shepherd replied, "Oh, only for the last thirty years, more or less. I have never tasted anything else except these herbs, which I have eaten once a day, and then I drink as much water as my food requires. The wages I receive from the owner of these sheep I give to the poor."

When the monk heard this, he bowed down at the feet of the shepherd and said, "I imagined that I had mastered abstinence, but you seem worthy of a greater reward than I. I have eaten every kind of green thing as soon as I found it."

Then the shepherd said to him calmly, "Now, it's not right that rational people should act like beasts. They should eat whatever is prepared for them with love, at the appropriate season, and afterwards fast from everything until the next appointed time."

The monk took the shepherd's words to heart, returned to his community, and applied them. He praised God and wondered how many unknown saints there were in the world.

—Story of the desert fathers, 4th–5th centuries, Egypt, from Palladius Hieronymus, 4th–5th centuries CE (*The Book of Paradise*).

Learning a New Alphabet

One time Abba Arsenius left the desert and went into a nearby village to ask an old man his thoughts about life.

Afterwards another brother asked the Abba about his trip. "You have so much learning, both Greek and Latin, yet you ask questions about the thoughts of this common villager?"

Abba Arsenius replied, "Yes, with Greek and Latin I am well acquainted, but I have not yet learned the alphabet of this villager."

—Story of the desert fathers, 4th–5th centuries, Egypt, from Palladius Hieronymus, 4th–5th centuries CE (*The Book of Paradise*).

Desert . . . Really?

The Arabs do not speak of desert or wilderness as we do. Why should they? To them it is neither desert nor wilderness, but a land of which they know every feature, a mother country whose smallest product has a use sufficient for their needs.

They know, or at least they knew in the days when their thoughts shaped themselves in deathless verse, how to rejoice in the great spaces and how to honor the rush of the storm.

In many a couplet they extolled the beauty of the watered spots. They sang of the fly that hummed there, just as those made glad with wine croon melodies for their own ears to hear. They sang of the pools of rain that shone like silver pieces, or gleamed dark as the warrior's mail when the wind ruffled them. They had watched, as they crossed the barren watercourses, the laggard wonders of the night, when the stars seemed chained to the sky as though the dawn would never come.

The ancient Arab poet Imru al-Qais had seen the Pleiades caught like jewels in the net of a girdle, and with the wolf that howled in the dark he had claimed fellowship: "You and I are of one family, and lo, the furrow that you plough and that I plough shall yield one harvest."

—Gertrude Bell, 1907 (*The Desert and the Sown: Travels in Palestine and Syria*), England.

The Crazed Communism of the Desert

People have looked upon the desert as barren land, the free-hold of whoever chose. But in fact each hill and valley had a person who was its acknowledged owner and would quickly assert the right of his or her family or clan to it, against aggression.

Even the wells and trees had their masters, who allowed people to make firewood of the one and drink of the other freely, as much as was required for their need, but who would instantly check anyone trying to turn the property to account and to exploit it or its products for private benefit.

The desert was held in a crazed communism by which nature and the elements were for the free use of every known friendly person for their own purposes and no more.

—T. E. Lawrence, 1922 (*Seven Pillars of Wisdom*),
England (in Arabia).

Prayers of Rabia

O God,
whatever you have designated as
my share of material things,
please give this to my enemies.
Whatever you have designated as
my share in the world to come,
please give this to my friends.
For me, you alone are enough.

***

O God,
my whole purpose here and
my whole desire
is to remember you.
My whole purpose
in the world to come
is to meet you.
That's what I can do on my side.
Now, please do with me as you wish.

> —Rabia al-Adawiyya, 8th century, Iraq,
> quoted by Fariduddin Attar, 12th century, Persia.

4

The Magic of Water

One Undivided Flow

Rocks and waters are words of God, and so are people. We all flow from one fountain-soul. All are expressions of one love.

God does not appear and flow out only from narrow chinks and round, bored wells, here and there in favored peoples and places.

God flows in grand, undivided currents, shoreless and boundless, over creeds and forms and all kinds of civilizations and peoples and beasts, saturating all and fountain-izing all.

—John Muir, 1872 (Letter), Scotland-USA.

Sometimes Boats Sink

The sea is no less beautiful to us because we know that sometimes boats sink. On the contrary, it is more beautiful. If she changed the movement of her waves to spare a boat, she would be a being of discernment and choice, not that fluid perfectly obeying all external pressures. It is this perfect obedience that is her beauty.

All the horrors that occur in this world are like the folds printed to the waves by gravity. That's why they lock up a beauty. Sometimes a poem, such as the *Iliad*, makes this beauty sensitive.

Matter is not beautiful when it obeys people, but only when it obeys God. If, in a work of art, it sometimes appears nearly as beautiful as the ocean, the mountains, or the flowers, it is because the light of God fills the artist.

For us, the obedience of things relates to God like the transparency of a windowpane relates to light. When we feel that obedience in our whole being, we see God.

—Simone Weil, 1942 (*Awaiting God*), France.

Too Smooth, Too Blue

It tossed and tossed
a little brig I knew.
O'ertook by blast
it spun and spun
and groped delirious, for morn.
It slipped and slipped,
as one that drunken stepped,
its white foot tripped,
then dropped from sight.
Ah, brig—good-night
to crew and you!
The ocean's heart
too smooth, too blue,
to break for you.

—Emily Dickinson, 1830–1886, USA.

This Life Is a Lake So Small

When cold masters water,
water becomes ice.
Another time it may turn to snow.
Three different things, or only one?
Like this, when the sun of
supreme consciousness shines fully,
these three—soul, nature, the supreme—
become the same.
By this sun all things,
whether with life or seemingly without it—
even the whole universe—
are seen as only Shiva.
This life is a lake so small,
there's no room for even
a mustard seed to grow.
Yet from this lake everyone drinks,
and into it fall deer, jackals,
rhinoceroses and sea-elephants.
Falling, falling, we are all falling—
almost before we have
time to be born.

—Lalla, 14th century CE, Kashmir.

The Foam and the Sea

The sea itself is one thing, the foam another.
Forget the foam for a moment and
open your eyes to the the sea.
Night and day, waves of foam rise from the sea.
You mistake the foam's ripples for the sea itself.
Like little boats we are tossed here and there.
We are blind though we are on the bright ocean.
O you who are asleep in the boat of the body,
you think you see the water!
Behold the water of waters!
Under the water, another water moves.
Within the spirit, a greater spirit calls.

—Jelaluddin Rumi, 13th century
(*Mathnawi*), Turkey.

A Long Soaking Rain

What things interest me at present?

A long, soaking rain, the drops trickling down the stubble, while I lay drenched on last year's bed of wild oats by the side of some bare hill, ruminating.

These things are of moment:

To watch this crystal globe just sent from heaven to associate with me. While these clouds and this somber, drizzling weather shut everyone else in, we two draw nearer and know one another.

The gathering in of the clouds with the last rush and dying breath of the wind. Then the regular dripping of twigs and leaves throughout the whole land. The impression of inward comfort and sociableness.

The drenched stubble and trees that drop beads on you as you pass, their dim outline seen through the rain on all sides, drooping in sympathy with yourself.

These are my undisputed territory.

—Henry David Thoreau, 1840 (Journals), USA.

How Much It Washes Away

Saw tracks of a shore bird—probably a sanderling, and followed them a little, then they turned toward the water and were soon obliterated by the sea. How much it washes away, and makes as though it had never been.

Time itself is like the sea, containing all that came before us, sooner or later sweeping us away on its flood and washing over and obliterating the traces of our presence, as the sea this morning erased the footprints of the bird.

—Rachel Carson, 1950–52 (Field Notebooks),
USA.

Inland

People that build their houses inland,
people that buy a plot of ground
shaped like a house, and build a house there,
far from the sea-board, far from the sound
of water sucking the hollow ledges,
tons of water striking the shore—
what do they long for, as I long for
one salt smell of the sea once more?
People the waves have not awakened,
spanking the boats at the harbor's head—
what do they long for, as I long for,
starting up in my inland bed,
beating the narrow walls, and finding
neither a window nor a door,
screaming to God for death by drowning—
one salt taste of the sea once more?

—Edna St. Vincent Millay, 1921, USA.

Goodness Like the Water

Water is peaceful and extends its beneficent action throughout nature, not even disdaining those gloomy depths that the vulgar look upon with horror, for water works much as the Tao does.

Now, the term *good* has a variety of applications. It may refer to the quality of ground upon which a house stands. Or to profundity in a thinker. Or to sincerity in a speaker. Or to a well-ordered government. Or to a capacity for accomplishing things, to punctuality, or other things.

But only when *goodness* is used in reference to freedom from conflict—like the water—can it be considered faultless.

—Lao Tze, 6th century BCE
(Tao Te Ching), China.

The Teaching of the Running River

Have you seen the tall mountains topped with snow?
Already the snow is melting away.
Have you heard the teaching of the running river?
It stays low to the ground as it flows away.
O Beloved, you are the most able one I see.
Everywhere I look, you are before me.
You're like a four-cornered tent
stretching, covering night and day.
All those great birds of knowledge in the sky—
why the sun doesn't burn them is a mystery.
The trees which give their fruit to us eternally—
even they don't stay long before they're passing away.
Our ocean is so deep you cannot dive it.
With a thousand words, still few understand it.
You can't leash a person who doesn't want it—
he'll break the leash and continue on his way.
Shah Hatayi's own heart is in these words—
but even the eyes of other dervishes he avoids.
His heart is tired, is drunk and sighs—
for all but his enemies' criticism passes away.

—Shah Hatayi (Ismail), 15th century,
Persia-Azerbaijan.

Water in the Basin

One of the Egyptian desert fathers told this story:

Once there were three monks who loved devotional service. They attempted the hardest penances and austerities they could find. After a while, they talked among themselves about what the most difficult thing to do would be, and each made a different decision. The first chose to travel around the world and, when he found conflict, tried to make peace. The second chose to constantly visit the sick. The third left for the desert so that he could live in quietness.

Finally, the first monk, who had chosen to resolve people's disputes with each other, found he was unable to create peace for everyone, and his spirit became sad. He found the monk who had chosen to visit the sick and found him also in anguish, because there were just too many sick people.

Then the two of them went off to find the monk in the desert. When they were together again they were very happy. The first two monks told the third of all the trouble they had found in the world and asked him to relate how his life in the desert had gone.

He was silent for a moment, but after a little he said, "Come on, let's fill a bucket with water from the well." After they had done that, the third monk said to the first two, "Now pour out some of the water into this deep basin and look down to the bottom." They did it.

"What do you see?" asked the third monk. They replied "We don't see anything of the bottom. There is too much silt."

After the water in the basin had ceased to move, the third monk said, "Ok, look again, now what do you see?"

"Now we see our own faces distinctly."

"That's the way it is," said the third monk. "Because of all the disturbances of the world, the one who dwells with others cannot see to the bottom of the bucket of the self, with all its hidden faults and virtues. Only if one lives in the peace and quiet of the desert, can one begin to see God clearly."

—Stories and sayings of the desert fathers,
3rd–4th centuries CE, Egypt, from
Palladius Hieronymus, 4th–5th centuries CE
(*The Book of Paradise*).

Stained Water

One day, when I was traveling through Idaho, I went into some woods. There I found a spring and a little pond covered with autumn leaves.

The water was stained red because of the red foliage. I was very thirsty, so I knelt down and scooped some water into my hands. The water was clear. It had not been stained or tinted by the autumn leaves.

Our mind, I realized, must be pure like this pond. The original nature of mind is not so far away. It can be attained immediately.

Purity is the nature of this original mind.

—Sokei-an Sasaki, 1935–39 (Lectures), Japan-USA.

Still Water

When water is still, it is like a mirror, reflecting your chin and eyebrows, everything. And if water obtains lucidity from stillness, how much more will the faculties of the mind do the same? The mind of the sage, being in repose, becomes the mirror of the universe, of all creation.

Repose, tranquility, stillness, inaction—these are the levels of the universe, the ultimate perfection of Tao. Therefore wise rulers and sages rest in these.

Repose, tranquility, stillness, inaction—these are the sources of all things. Hold to this when coming forward to pacify a troubled world.

Your merit will be great, your name illustrious, and the empire united into one.

In your repose you will be wise. In your movements, powerful. By inaction you will gain honor, and by confining yourself to what's pure and simple, you will prevent the whole world from struggling with you just for appearance's sake.

—Chuang Tzu, 4th century BCE, China

The Book of the River

The face of the water, in time, became a wonderful book—a book that was a dead language to the uneducated passenger, but which told its mind to me without reserve, delivering its most cherished secrets as clearly as if it uttered them with a voice.

And it was not a book to be read once and thrown aside, for it had a new story to tell every day. Throughout the long twelve hundred miles there was never a page that was void of interest, never one that you could leave unread without loss, never one that you would want to skip, thinking you could find higher enjoyment in some other thing.

There never was so wonderful a book written by anyone. Never one whose interest was so absorbing, so unflagging, so sparklingly renewed with every re-perusal.

The passenger who could not read it was charmed with a peculiar sort of faint dimple on its surface (on the rare occasions when he did not overlook it altogether). But to the pilot of a steamboat that was an italicized passage. Indeed it was more than that, it was a legend of the largest CAPITALS, with a string of shouting exclamation points at the end of it, for it meant that a wreck or a rock was buried there that could tear the life out of the strongest vessel that ever floated. It is the faintest and simplest expression the water ever makes, and the most hideous to a pilot's eye.

In truth, the passenger who could not read this book saw nothing but all manner of pretty pictures in it painted by the sun and shaded by the clouds, whereas to the trained eye these were not pictures at all, but the grimmest and most dead-earnest of reading-matter.

Now when I had mastered the language of this water and had come to know every trifling feature that bordered the great river as familiarly as I knew the letters of the alphabet, I had made a valuable acquisition. But I had lost something, too. I had lost something that could never be restored to me while I lived. All the grace, the beauty, the poetry had gone out of the majestic river!

I still keep in mind a certain wonderful sunset that I witnessed when steamboating was new to me.

A broad expanse of the river was turned to blood. In the middle distance, the red hue brightened into gold, through which a solitary log came floating, black and conspicuous. In one place a long, slanting mark lay sparkling upon the water. In another the surface was broken by boiling, tumbling rings, that were as many-tinted as an opal. Where the ruddy flush was faintest was a smooth spot that was covered with graceful circles and radiating lines, ever so delicately traced. The shore on our left was densely wooded, and the somber shadow that fell from this forest was broken in one place by a long, ruffled trail that shone like silver. And high above the forest wall a clean-stemmed dead tree waved a single leafy bough that glowed like a flame in the unobstructed splendor that was flowing from the sun.

There were graceful curves, reflected images, woody heights, soft distances. And over the whole scene, far and near, the dissolving lights drifted steadily, enriching it every passing moment with new marvels of coloring. I stood like one bewitched. I drank it in, in a speechless rapture. The world was new to me, and I had never seen anything like this at home.

But as I have said, a day came when I began to cease from noting the glories and the charms that the moon and the sun and the twilight wrought upon the river's face. Another day came when I ceased altogether to note them. Then, if that sunset scene had been repeated, I should have looked upon it without rapture, and should have commented upon it, inwardly, after this fashion:

This sun means that we are going to have wind tomorrow. That floating log means that the river is rising, small thanks to it. That slanting mark on the water refers to a bluff reef that is going to kill somebody's steamboat one of these nights if it keeps on stretching out like that. Those tumbling boils show a dissolving bar and a changing channel there. The lines and circles in the slick water over yonder are a warning that that troublesome place is shoaling up dangerously. That silver streak in the shadow of the forest is the break from a new snag, and it has located itself in the very best place it could have found to fish for steamboats. That tall dead tree, with a single living branch, is not going to last long, and then how is a body ever going to get through this blind place at night without the friendly old landmark?

No, the romance and the beauty were all gone from the river. All the value any feature of it had for me now was the amount of usefulness it could furnish toward compassing the safe piloting of a steamboat.

—Mark Twain, 1883 (*Life on the Mississippi*), USA.

Sliding Like a Shadow

In fording a swollen stream, one's strongest sensation is of the pouring strength of the water against one's limbs. The effort to poise the body against it gives significance to this simple act of walking through running water.

Early in the season the water may be so cold that one has no sensation except of cold. The whole being retracts itself, uses all its resources to endure this icy delight. But in heat the freshness of the water slides over the skin like shadow. The whole skin has this delightful sensitivity. It feels the sun, it feels the wind running inside one's garment, it feels water closing on it as one slips under—the catch in the breath, like a wave held back, the glow that releases one's entire cosmos, running to the ends of the body as the spent wave runs out upon the sand.

This plunge into the cold water of a mountain pool seems for a brief moment to disintegrate the very self. It is not to be borne: one is lost: stricken: annihilated. Then life pours back.

—Nan Shepherd, 1947
(*The Living Mountain*), Scotland.

The White River at Nan-yang

Wading at dawn to the White River's source,
severed awhile from the ways of people,
to islands tinged with the colors of paradise,
where the river sky drowns in limpid space.
While my eyes were watching
the clouds that travel to the sea,
my heart was as idle as
the fish that swim in the stream.
With long singing,
I put the sun to rest.
Riding the moonlight,
I returned to my fields and home.

—Li Bai, 8th century CE, China.

5

Wild
Companions

Fish Running in Our Veins

The fish are going up the brooks that open after the winter freeze.

They are dispersing themselves through the fields and woods, imparting new life into them. They are taking their places under the shelving banks and in the dark swamps. The water running down meets the fish running up. They hear the latest news.

Spring-aroused fish are running up our veins too. Little fish are seeking the sources of the brooks, seeking to disseminate their principles.

Talk about a revival of religion, and businessmen's prayer-meetings, with which all the country goes mad now! What if they were as true and wholesome a revival as the little fish feel that come out of the sluggish waters and run up the brooks toward their sources?

—Henry David Thoreau, 1858 (Journals), USA.

The Joy of Fish

Chuang Tzu was walking with his friend Hui Tzu in the forest one day. They were talking about living forever. Hui Tzu was convinced that one could concoct herbal remedies combined with small amounts of poisonous minerals that would ensure a person's immortality.

"Why bother with all that?" asked Chuang Tzu. "We are already immortal, part of the never-ending, never-beginning Tao. Why ingest all these poisons? Just live your life according to the Tao, and immortality will appear on its own."

"I disagree," responded Hui Tzu. "If that were true, every idiot would be immortal."

"Exactly," said Chuang Tzu.

Later that day, they were walking over a small stream spanned by a moon bridge.

"Look at these fish," said Chuang Tzu, pointing below him as he sat down on the bridge, dangling his feet into the water. "They are so relaxed as they swim around. This is the joy of fish."

"How can you know what fish enjoy?" asked Hui Tzu truculently. "Impossible!"

"You are not me, so how can you know what I know about the joy of fish?" replied Chuang Tzu.

"All right, I am not you," exclaimed Hui Tzu in aggravation. "But you are not a fish, either!"

"Just so," said Chuang Tzu, his fingers stroking the water as the fish came up to nibble them. "But when you asked me how can I know what fish enjoy, you already knew that I knew. The how was by walking over the river."

—Story of Chuang Tzu, 4th century BCE, China.

The Philosophy of a Flea

If a flea could use reason,
and if it could use it to explore
the eternal abyss of divine being
out of which it originally came,
then all the ideas, ideals and images of "God"
it could discover couldn't make it any happier.
Therefore, we pray to be done
with these "God"-images and instead
allow the truth to break us back
through into that eternity
where the highest angel, the flea and the soul
already are the same in one truth:
where "I" was at the first beginning,
when "I" wanted what "I" was,
and "I" was what "I" wanted.

—Meister Eckhart, 13th–14th CE, Germany.

The Fun of Other Creatures

Surely all God's people, however serious and savage, great or small, like to play.

Whales and elephants; dancing, humming gnats, and invisibly small mischievous microbes—all are warm with divine radium and must have lots of fun in them.

—John Muir, 1913 (*The Story of My Boyhood and Youth*), Scotland-USA.

A Cat Does Not Use Chopsticks

You must not think that original nature destroys laws.

It enters water and fire, and observes the law of water and of fire and of New York.

When it enters the human being and the cat and dog, it observes the law of the human being and the cat and dog. When it enters the cat, the cat does not use chopsticks—dishes are used with chopsticks. When it enters the Japanese, the Japanese uses the chopsticks. In an American, it will use a knife and fork.

Why should there be a fixed law?

—Sokei-an Sasaki, 1935–39 (Lectures), Japan-USA.

Worm Democracy

Do not think that by praying with deep devotion you are greater than anyone else. You are like any other creature, created for the sake of the worship of the Holy One, blessed be that One.

God gave a mind to the other creatures just as God gave you a mind.

What makes you superior to a worm? The worm serves the creator with all its mind and strength! Humans too are worms and maggots, as it is written in Psalm 22 "I am a worm and no human being."

If God had not given you intelligence, you would not be able to worship God except like a worm.

Bear in mind that you, the worm, and all other small creatures are considered equals in the world, for God created everything and everyone and gave us all the abilities we have.

Always keep this matter in mind.

—Baal Shem Tov, 18th century, Poland.

The Bee of the Soul

Traversing the fields,
a bee gathers the ingredients for honey.
Traversing the ages,
the soul infuses sweetness into the mind.
The stars are hidden when the sun rises,
and thoughts vanish when
the intellect returns to its own realm.
Raindrops moisten the furrows,
just as tear-laden sighs,
rising from the heart,
soften the soul's state during prayer.
Simply speaking of the laws of nature
arouses deep admiration.
But when they are fully understood,
they are like fields full of flowers,
whose lavish blossoms give out
a spiritual sweetness like nectar from heaven.
Bees surround their queen
among fresh meadow-flowers.
And angelic powers surround and assist
a soul that is constantly in a
state of loving concentration,
for the soul is kindred to them.

—Ilias the Presbyter, 11th century (*The Philokalia*) Turkey.

The Bees of the Invisible

Nature and all of the objects of our daily use are preliminary and frail. As long as we are here, however, they are our possession and our friendship, accessories to our suffering and joy, just as they had been the intimates of our predecessors.

It is thus our task not only not to malign and take down everything that is here but rather, because of the transience that we have in common with it, to comprehend and transform with an innermost consciousness these appearances and things.

Transform? Yes, for it is our task to impress this provisional, transient earth upon ourselves so deeply, so agonizingly, and so passionately that its essence rises up again "invisibly" within us.

We are the bees of the invisible. We ceaselessly gather the honey of the visible to store it in the great golden hive of the invisible.

—Rainer Maria Rilke, 1925 (Letters),
Austria-Bohemia (now Czech Republic).

The Heaven of the Crickets

First observe the creak of crickets. The song of only one alone is most interesting to me. It suggests lateness, but only as we come to a knowledge of eternity after some acquaintance with time.

It is only late for all trivial and hurried pursuits. It suggests a mature wisdom, never late, being above all temporal considerations, which possesses the coolness and maturity of autumn amidst the aspiration of spring and the heats of summer.

To the birds they say, "Ah! You speak like children from impulse. Nature speaks through you, but with us it is ripe knowledge. The seasons do not revolve for us, we sing their lullaby."

So they chant, eternal, at the roots of the grass.

It is heaven where they are, and their dwelling does not need to be lifted up. Forever the same, in May and in November.

Serenely wise, their song has the security of prose. They have drunk no wine but the dew. It is no transient love-strain, hushed when the incubating season is past, but a glorifying of God and enjoying of God forever.

They sit aside from the revolution of the seasons. Their strain is as unvaried as truth.

Only in their saner moments do people hear the crickets. It is balm to philosophers and tempers their thoughts.

In their song they ignore our accidents. They are not concerned about the news. They have begun a manuscript that does not pause for any news, for it knows only the eternal.

—Henry David Thoreau, 1854 (Journals), USA.

The Sensitive Horse

Animals can be very sensitive to the world of the soul.

When Saint Spiridon, a bishop of Cyprus in the third century, was on his way to the ecumenical council, he stayed overnight in a hostel.

The monk who accompanied him came into their room after checking on the horses and said, "Father, I can't understand why our horse doesn't eat the cabbage I just bought from the owner of the hostel."

"Because," replied the saint, "the animal feels the intolerable stench of this particular cabbage. That comes from the fact that the owner is infected with obsessive stinginess. One who is not enlightened in spirit does not notice this, but the saints and many animals have the gift of God to recognize such things."

—Father Varsonofy of Optina, 19th century, Russia.

The Price of Tears

Once a dervish was wandering through the desert when he met a tribal leader, who was sitting by the side of the road weeping.

"Why are you crying?" asked the dervish.

"Look at my poor dog!" exclaimed the tribesman. "It's dying. It comforted me in my loneliness. It drove away thieves, and it was a skilled hunter as well. Now it's dying!"

"But what's the matter with it?," asked the dervish. "Was it wounded, is it sick?"

"No, it is simply dying of hunger. Here we are in the middle of the desert, after all."

The dervish saw that the man had a shoulder bag that looked full.

"Excuse me, honored sir, what's that in your bag?" the dervish asked.

"Bread, and the leftovers of last night's meal."

"So why don't you give some to your dog?!"

"My love and charity don't reach that far. Even if we found somewhere to buy bread in the desert, it would cost money. Tears are free."

"You're a water-bag full of wind!" exclaimed the dervish. "Anyone who values a crust of bread more than tears is a fool."

—A story told by Jelaluddin Rumi,
13th century, Turkey.

Earth-Born Companions

Why should human beings value themselves as more than a small part of the one great unit of creation? And what creature of all that the Lord has taken the pains to make is not essential to the completeness of that unit—the cosmos? The universe would be incomplete without human beings, but it would also be incomplete without the smallest submicroscopic creature that dwells beyond our conceitful eyes and knowledge.

From the dust of the earth, from the common elementary fund, the creator has made homo sapiens. From the same material the creator has made every other creature, however noxious and insignificant to us. They are earth-born companions and our fellow mortals.

This star, our own good earth, made many a successful journey around the heavens before human beings were made, and whole realms of creatures enjoyed existence and returned to dust before humans appeared to claim them.

After human beings have played their part in creation's plan, they may also disappear without any general burning or extraordinary commotion whatever.

—John Muir, 1916 (*A Thousand-Mile Walk to the Gulf*), Scotland-USA.

Wild Swans

I looked in my heart while the wild swans went over.
And what did I see I had not seen before?
Only a question less or a question more.
Nothing to match the flight of wild birds flying.
Tiresome heart, forever living and dying,
house without air, I leave you and lock your door.
Wild swans, come over the town, come over
the town again, trailing your legs and crying!

— Edna St. Vincent Millay, 1921, USA.

The Voice of the Wood Thrush

As I come over the hill, I hear the wood thrush singing its evening lay.

This is the only bird whose note affects me like music, affects the flow and tenor of my thought, my fancy and imagination. It lifts and exhilarates me. It is inspiring. It is a medicinal tonic to my soul. It is an elixir to my eyes and a fountain of youth to all my senses. It changes all hours to an eternal morning. It banishes all trivialness.

I long for wildness, a nature that I cannot put my foot through. Woods where the wood thrush forever sings, where the hours are early morning ones, and there is dew on the grass, and the day is forever unproved.

Where I might have a fertile unknown for soil around me.

—Henry David Thoreau, 1852 (Journals), USA.

Dances with Swifts

[W]e were standing on the edge of an outward facing precipice, when I was startled by a whizzing sound behind me.

Something dark swished past the side of my head at a speed that made me giddy. Hardly had I got back my balance when it came again, whistling through the windless air, which eddied round me with the motion. This time my eyes were ready, and I realised that a swift was sweeping in mighty curves over the edge of the plateau, plunging down the face of the rock and rising again like a jet of water.

No one had told me I should find swifts on the mountain. Eagles and ptarmigan, yes: but that first sight of the mad, joyous abandon of the swift over and over the very edge of the precipice shocked me with a thrill of elation. All that volley of speed, those convolutions of delight, to catch a few flies!

The discrepancy between purpose and performance made me laugh aloud—a laugh that gave the same feeling of release as though I had been dancing for a long time.

—Nan Shepherd, 1947
(*The Living Mountain*), Scotland.

The Dragon of the Black Pool

Deep are the waters of the Black Pool, colored like ink. They say a Holy Dragon lives there, which people have never seen.

Beside the pool people have built a shrine, and the authorities have established a ritual.

A dragon by itself remains a dragon, only people can make it a god. Prosperity and disaster, rain and drought, plagues and pestilences—all these the village people regard as the Holy Dragon's doing. They make offerings of suckling-pig and pour libations of wine. The nature of the morning prayers and evening gifts depends on the resident medium's advice, for instance:

"When the dragon comes . . . Ah!
The wind stirs and sighs.
Throw paper money . . . Ah!
Wave silk umbrellas.
When the dragon goes . . . Ah!
The wind also still.
Incense-fire dies . . . Ah!
The cups and vessels must be cold.
Stack meat on the rocks of the pool's shore.
Let wine flow on the grass in front of the shrine."

I do not know, of all these offerings, how much the Holy Dragon eats, but the mice of the woods and the foxes of the hills are continually drunk and sated.

Why are the foxes so lucky?

And what have the suckling-pigs done that, year by year, they should be killed, merely to glut the foxes?

The foxes are robbing the Holy Dragon and eating its suckling-pig. Beneath the ninefold depths of its pool, does the Dragon know or not?

—Bai Juyi, 8th–9th century CE, China.

6

Speaking Wildly in Society

Roots and Needs

A fellow philosopher saw Socrates gnawing on the root of a tree and said to him condescendingly,

"If you served someone rich and powerful as I do, you wouldn't need to eat food like that!"

"If you could eat food like this," responded Socrates, "then you wouldn't need to serve the rich and powerful."

—Story of Socrates, 5th century BCE, Greece.

Sliding Off the Earth's Shoulders

We play with dark forces that cannot be captured with the names we give them, like children playing with fire.

And it seems for a moment as if all energy had rested dormant in all objects until now, until we arrived to apply it to our fleeting life and its requirements. But, again and again throughout millennia, those forces shake off their names and rise like an oppressed class against their little masters, or not even against them—they simply rise and the various cultures slide off the shoulders of the earth, which is once again great and expansive and alone with its oceans, trees, and stars.

What does it mean that we transform the outermost surface of the earth, that we groom its forests and meadows and extract coal and minerals from its crust, that we receive the fruits from the trees as if they were meant for us?

If we were only to recall even a single hour when nature acted beyond us, beyond our hopes, beyond our lives, with that sublime highness and indifference that fill all of its gestures. It knows nothing of us. And whatever human beings might have accomplished, not one has yet reached such greatness that nature shared in their pain or would have joined in their rejoicing.

—Rainer Maria Rilke, 1902 (Letters),
Austria-Bohemia (now Czech Republic).

Loafing

If a man walked in the woods for love of them half of each day, he is in danger of being regarded as a loafer.

But if he spends his whole day as a speculator, shearing off those woods and making earth bald before her time, he is esteemed an industrious and enterprising citizen.

As if a town had no interest in its forests but to cut them down!

—Henry David Thoreau, 1863
(*Life without Principle*), USA.

Straight Hook

There was a fisherman in China who for forty years used a straight needle to fish with.

When someone asked him, "Why don't you use a bent hook?" The fisherman replied, "You can catch ordinary fish with a bent hook, but I will catch a great fish with my straight needle."

Word of this came to the ear of the emperor, so he went to see this fool of a fisherman for himself. The emperor asked the fisherman, "What are you fishing for?"

The fisherman replied, "I am fishing for you, emperor!"

If you have no experience in fishing with the straight needle, you cannot understand this story. Simply, I am holding my arms on my breast. Like that fisherman with the straight needle, I fish for you good fishes. I do not circulate letters. I do not advertise. I do not ask you to come. I do not ask you to stay. I do not entertain you. You come, and I am living my own life.

If you fish with the straight needle, life is easy, and there is no danger of your hooking yourself.

—Sokei-An Sasaki,
1930–1941 (Lectures), Japan-USA.

Greeting a Governor

Once a local Egyptian governor determined to go see Abba Simon in his desert community. When the old man heard about this, he quickly left his cell and went up a palm tree to clean it. When the governor's retinue arrived, a servant called out to him, "Old man, can you tell us where the famous monk Abba Simon might be?" Abba Simon called down to them, "That person is not here." So they departed.

The governor tried again, and this time arranged to see Abba Simon through his fellow monastics. They told him, "Please, Father, he will just keep coming. Make yourself ready. This governor has heard of your life and works, and he just wishes to come and be blessed by you."

The old man replied, "All right, I am ready."

Then the old man took some bread and cheese in his hand, started eating them greedily and went out to the door. He sat down near the threshold and fidgeted about, changing from place to place, still eating. When the governor arrived with his company, he saw this spectacle and was disgusted. "So this is the famous ascetic monk of whom we have heard!" he said huffily. They all left Abba Simon in peace after that.

—Story of the desert fathers, 4th–5th centuries,
Egypt, from Palladius Hieronymus,
4th–5th centuries CE (*The Book of Paradise*).

The Purpose of a Shepherd

Once a solitary dervish had taken up residence in an out-of-the way corner of a desert. By and by, a king passed by. Because contentment is the enjoyment of any domain, the dervish did not raise his head, nor show the king the least sign of attention. And because, as ruling is all about appearances and pride, the king took offense.

The king said to his vizier, "This tribe of ragged beggars resembles nothing more than brute beasts and doesn't possess either grace or good manners."

Taking the cue, the vizier stepped up to the dervish and proclaimed, "O lucky man! The sovereign of the universe has just passed by you. Why didn't you pay him homage, and at least bow a bit in respect?"

The dervish answered, "Please tell your sovereign: expect service from a person who wants to court your favor. Let him know that kings are meant for the protection of the people, and not the people for the honoring of kings. Though it be for the people's benefit that his glory is exalted, yet the king is but the shepherd of the poor. The sheep are not intended for the service of the shepherd, but the shepherd is appointed to tend the sheep.

"Today you see one man proud from prosperity, another with a heart sore from adversity. Wait a few days until the dust of the grave consumes the brain of your vain, foolish head.

When the record of destiny comes into effect, the distinction between ruler and subject disappears. Were people to turn over the dust of the dead, could they distinguish that of the rich ones from the poor?"

These sayings made a strong impression upon the king. He walked over to the dervish and said, "Ask me for something."

The dervish replied, "What I desire is that you don't trouble me again!"

The king then said, "Please favor me with a piece of advice."

The dervish answered, "Attend to your people now that the good things of life are in your hands. For wealth and power pass quickly from one hand to another."

— Saadi Shirazi, 13th century CE
(*The Rose Garden*), Persia (now Iran).

The Victim Ox

In the 4th century BCE, King Wei of Chu heard of the wisdom of Chuang Tzu and sent messengers with expensive gifts to bring him to his court. He promised that he would make Chuang Tzu his chief minister.

Chuang Tzu said to the messengers, "These thousand ounces of silver you brought would be a great gain, and to be a high noble and minister is a most honorable position. But haven't you seen the victim-ox for the ritual sacrifice? It is carefully fed for several years, and robed with rich embroidery so that it's fit to enter the Grand Temple. When the time comes for it to do so, it would prefer to be an undistinguished little pig. But by then there is no hope for that."

"Go away and leave me in peace! I would rather enjoy myself in the middle of a filthy ditch than be subject to the rules and restrictions of the court of a sovereign. I have determined never to take office, but prefer the enjoyment of my own free will."

—Story of Chuang Tzu, 4th century BCE, China.

The Proper Influence

Once, in the late 4th century, the archbishop of Alexandria visited the desert community of Scete, located in the desolate Nitrian desert in northern Egypt.

At the time, the community was home to Abba Pambo, who always tried to follow the words of David's Psalm 39: "We human beings who walk are only a shadow, a reflection, and piling up wealth is as ephemeral as a puff of wind." He mostly worked all day and said very little. When his fellow brothers would ask him a question, he would only answer after pausing for silence and prayer.

Before the archbishop arrived, the brothers gathered together and said urgently to Abba Pambo, "Won't you please say some wise words to the bishop, so that he will support us here?"

After his customary long pause, the old man replied, "If my silence doesn't help us, my words certainly will not."

On his deathbed, they say that Abba Pambo's face shone like lightning, as did the face of Moses after his experience with the burning bush, and he said, "I am going to my Lord as one who has not yet begun to serve."

—Story of the desert fathers, 4th–5th centuries,
Egypt, from Palladius Hieronymus,
4th–5th centuries CE (*The Book of Paradise*).

From Dervish to King (and Back Again)

Once a king reached the end of his days and had no heir to succeed him. He made a will that stated, "You will place my crown on the head of whichever person first enters the city gate in the morning and commit the kingdom to this person's charge."

It just so happened that the first person that presented himself at the city gate was a poor dervish, who had passed his whole life living from hand to mouth and patching rags.

Reluctantly the ministers of state and nobles of the court fulfilled the conditions of the old king's will and laid the keys of the treasury and citadel at the dervish's feet.

For a while the dervish governed the kingdom peacefully, until inevitably some of the nobles got fed up with egalitarianism. The princes of the various territories raised armies and rose to oppose him. In short order those loyal to the dervish were routed, and several of his provinces taken from him.

The dervish was hurt to his soul by these events. He had only tried to do his best. When one of his old dervish friends returned from a long journey and found him in such dignity, he exclaimed, "Wow!" Which in those less hurried and more articulate days, he expressed something like this:

"Thanks be to the Allah, lord of majesty and glory, that such lofty fortune has comforted you and that prosperity was your guide. Roses have grown from your thorns, and the thorns were extracted from your feet, and now you have arrived at this elevated rank! As Holy Qur'an says, with hardship comes ease, and joy replaces sorrow. In one season, a plant is in flower and at another, all withered. The tree is at one moment naked and at another richly clothed with leaves."

The dervish replied, "My dear friend, don't congratulate me, only offer condolences. When you last saw me I had no thought but to get the day's crumb of bread. Now I have the cares of a whole kingdom on my head!"

Saadi comments:

If the world opposes us, we are victims of pain. If prosperous, we find ourselves in luxury's chains. In this life, no calamity is more afflicting, no fortune more risky, than the one that upsets our hearts.

If you want wealth, don't ask for contentment. Should a rich person throw money in your lap, beware! Don't think of it as a benefit. Wise people say that the patience of the poor is worth more than the gifts of the rich. The famous Persian prince Bahram Ghor had seven princesses as consorts, each living in separate palaces devoted to the seven planets. They taught him the facts of life—how wonderful! But if he were to throw a banquet for them all, including his whole court, it would not ultimately be worth the gift of a locust's leg from one ant to another.

—Story told by Saadi Shirazi, 13th century CE
(*The Rose Garden*), Persia (now Iran).

The Problem with Responsibility

Once a Taoist monk decided to test his enlightenment by moving from the mountains to the city. When he was halfway there, he turned back and met his master on the road.

"Why are you returning?" asked the master.

"On my way, I stopped at an inn," replied his student. "While there I noticed that the innkeeper honored me more than his other guests."

"And that was a problem?" inquired the master.

"Yes," replied the monk. "When a person is not stable in realization, a charismatic aura will leak out of him like a fog and make an impression on the hearts of other people, who then begin to honor him. I imagined what would happen if I went to the city and were noticed by nobles or politicians. They would notice me, offer me positions, and try to give me responsibilities. I didn't want that. I want to remain free, and so I am returning to the mountains.

"That's a good way to look at it," said the master. "But even if you stay in the mountains at our monastery, the same thing might happen. Others will still try to give you honor and responsibilities."

Later, back at the monastery, the master visited the monk and found many shoes outside the door of his cell. There was a circle of young students gathered around the monk, listening eagerly as he lectured to them. The master peeked in the door and immediately turned to leave. The student saw and ran after him.

"Did you want to offer me a blessing, master?" asked the monk.

"No!" yelled the master. "I told you that others would try to give you responsibilities. The problem is not that you allow them to do it, but that you are not able to prevent them from doing so! It is no use having such an effect on people if it disturbs your inner peace.

"If you unbalance your original nature, it will not help you and will invalidate the teaching you offer."

—Lie Yukou, 4th century BCE
(*Liezi* Taoist collection), China.

Common Everyday Beauty

Fresh beauty opens one's eyes wherever it is really seen, but the very abundance and completeness of the common beauty that besets our steps prevent it being absorbed and appreciated.

It is a good thing, therefore, to make short excursions now and then to the bottom of the sea among dulse and coral, or up among the clouds on mountain-tops, or in balloons, or even to creep like worms into dark holes and caverns underground, not only to learn something of what is going on in those out-of-the-way places, but to see better what the sun sees on our return to common, everyday beauty.

—John Muir, 1894 (*The Mountains of California*),
Scotland-USA.

Writing from the Earth

Write often, write upon a thousand themes, rather than long at a time, not trying to turn too many feeble somersaults in the air—and so come down upon your head at last. Antæus-like, be not long absent from the ground.

Those sentences are good and well discharged that are like so many little resiliencies from the spring floor of our life—a distinct fruit and kernel itself, springing from terra firma.

Let there be as many distinct plants as the soil and the light can sustain. Take as many bounds in a day as possible. Sentences uttered with your back to the wall.

—Henry David Thoreau, 1851 (Journals), USA.

Returning Home

I rushed here and there, longing,
seeking and searching, day and night.
At last I returned home and found
what I was looking for—the guru inside!
Like grasping a star, I held on.
Controlling my breath,
like fanning a flame with a bellows,
my heart-lamp came alight.
Breathing on that light,
the chaff that separates me
from my true nature scattered.
Now even in darkness
that light holds me tight.
Go ahead, rule a kingdom—no rest there.
Give it away—your heart's still troubled.
Only free your soul from desire—
the soul that never dies!
Better yet, while alive, die.
Then you'll know the truth.
Your reputation is like water
carried in a basket.
If you can hold the wind in your hand
or leash an elephant with your hair—
sure, then you can hold onto it!

—Lalla, 14th century, Kashmir.

Living in the Mountains with Crowds

There are hermits living in the mountains
who behave as if they live in the town.
They are wasting their time.
One can be single and unified in one's mind
while living in a crowd.
Likewise solitary hermits can live in a
crowd of their personal thoughts.

—Amma Syncletica, 4th century CE, Egypt.

The Flower Market

In the royal city, spring is almost over—
tinkle, tinkle—the coaches and horses pass.
We tell each other, "This is the peony season,"
and follow the crowd that goes to the flower market.
"Cheap and dear—no uniform price!" cries the hawker.
"The cost of the plant depends on the number of blossoms.
For a fine flower, a hundred pieces of damask.
For a cheap flower, five bits of silk.
When planting, spread an awning to protect them,
then weave a wattle-fence to screen them.
If you sprinkle water and cover the roots with mud,
when they are transplanted, they will keep their beauty."
Each household thoughtlessly follows the custom,
one by one, no one realizing the consequences.
An old farm laborer happened to be passing by.
He bowed his head and sighed deeply.
But no one understood this sigh. It meant:
"A cluster of these expensive, deep-red flowers
would pay the taxes of ten poor houses."

—Bai Juyi, 8th–9th century CE, China.

The Real World

The pleasures, the values of contact with the natural world, are not reserved for the scientists. They are available to anyone who will place himself under the influence of a lonely mountaintop—or the sea—or the stillness of a forest; or who will stop to think about so small a thing as the mystery of a growing seed.

I am not afraid of being thought a sentimentalist when I stand here tonight and tell you that I believe natural beauty has a necessary place in the spiritual development of any individual or any society. I believe that whenever we destroy beauty, or whenever we substitute something man-made and artificial for a natural feature of the earth, we have retarded some part of man's spiritual growth.

I believe this affinity of the human spirit for the earth and its beauties is deeply and logically rooted. As human beings, we are part of the whole stream of life. We have been human beings for perhaps a million years. But life itself passes on something of itself to other life—that mysterious entity that moves and is aware of itself and its surroundings, and so is distinguished from rocks or senseless clay—[from which] life arose many hundreds of millions of years ago. Since then it has developed, struggled, adapted itself to its surroundings, evolved an infinite number of forms. But its living protoplasm is built of the same elements as air, water, and rock. To these the mysterious spark of life was added.

Our origins are of the earth. And so there is in us a deeply seated response to the natural universe, which is part of our humanity.

—Rachel Carson, 1954 (Lecture), USA.

7

Reading
the Book
of Nature

Nature's First Book

The first book given by God to rational beings was the nature of creation.

Written teachings were only added later, after we began to make mistakes.

—Isaac of Nineveh, 7th century CE, Eastern Arabia.

Nature Is What We See . . .

"Nature" is what we see—
the hill, the afternoon,
squirrel, eclipse, the bumble-bee.
Nay, nature is heaven.
Nature is what we hear—
the bobolink, the sea,
thunder, the cricket.
Nay, Nature is harmony.
Nature is what we know
but have no art to say,
so impotent our wisdom is
to her simplicity.

—Emily Dickinson, 1830–1886, USA.

Falling Like Fragrant Dew

The Tao is unchanging and has no name.

Although this statement is short and simple, the world cannot grasp it. Yet if rulers were only to receive it, nothing under heaven would not yield to them. The Tao would produce a spirit of harmony that would unite heaven and earth and fall like a fragrant dew upon everything. Then people would no longer need to receive orders from others, but would be fully aware of what is right to do and when, capable of controlling their own actions.

But when a name was given to this Great First Cause, a naming that has continued to this day, this harmonious knowledge I speak of became arrested. And soon we no longer recognize what is withheld from us.

Ah! If the right knowledge of this reality were only to spread through the land, it would become like the ocean and great rivers into which all the smaller brooks and streams continuously flow.

—Lao Tze, 4th–6th century BCE
(Tao Te Ching), China.

You Cause Our Rivers to Flow

You are hidden from us
though the heavens are filled with your light,
which is brighter than the sun and moon.
You are hidden, yet reveal our hidden secrets.
You are the source that causes our rivers to flow.
You are hidden in your essence, but seen by your gifts.
You are the water, and we the millstone.
You are the wind, and we the dust.
The wind is unseen, but the dust is seen by all.
You are the spring, and we the sweet, green garden.
Spring is not seen, only its gifts.
You are like the soul, we like the hand and foot.
Soul tells hand and foot to hold, take, and walk.
You are reason, we are the tongue.
Reason teaches the tongue to speak.
You are the joy, and we are the laughing.
Laughter only arises from joy.
Our every motion, every moment, bears witness
proving the presence of the Oneness
that ever arises and stands.

—Jelaluddin Rumi, 13th century (*Mathnawi*), Turkey.

A Storm of Beauty

When we contemplate the whole globe
as one great dewdrop,
striped and dotted with
continents and islands,
flying through space
with other stars, all singing and
shining together as one,
the whole universe appears as
an infinite storm of beauty.

—John Muir, 1915 (*Travels in Alaska*),
Scotland-USA.

The World Stands Out

The world stands out on either side
no wider than the heart is wide.
Above the world is stretched the sky
no higher than the soul is high.
The heart can push the sea and land
farther away on either hand.
The soul can split the sky in two,
and let the face of God shine through.
But East and West will pinch the heart
that cannot keep them pushed apart.
And he whose soul is flat—the sky
will cave in on him by and by.

—Edna St. Vincent Millay, 1917, USA.

Talk of Mysteries

Talk of mysteries!
Think of our life in nature.
Daily to be shown matter,
to come in contact with it—
rocks, trees, wind on our cheeks!
The solid earth!
The actual world!
The common sensing!
Contact! Contact!
Who are we?
Where are we?

—Henry David Thoreau, 1848
(*The Maine Woods*), USA.

Free of Excess

The essence of your nature is
free of any excess.
It pervades the entire universe.
If this is the nature of the highest reality,
who is the object of worship?
And whom are we trying to pacify?
Waves arise from water,
flames from fire and
light rays from the sun.
So the waves of reality,
from which emanate the universe,
are our real source.

—Vijnana Bhairava Tantra,
12th century CE, Kashmir.

Accepting Original Purity

Earth is not impure. Water is not impure. Neither is fire nor air impure. So your body is not impure. Nothing is impure.

Why do you feel this impurity?

Because your mind is impure. Your mind is still sleeping. If your mind is not pure, you really cannot see the pure world. You cannot accept this human body, and when you cannot accept this human body, you do not obey the law of the human body.

—Sokei-an Sasaki, 1935–39 (Lectures), Japan-USA.

The Next Heap of Grass

The same rock can anchor a throne
or fix a pavement.
Really, it is all just part of the earth.
You could find a millstone around your neck
or a mill inside that grinds grain.
Consider this:
Shiva is very hard to find!
You are the heavens,
you alone the earth,
the day, the night, the air itself.
You are the *prasad*, the anointed sandal,
the flowers offered, the holy water sprinkled.
Since you are everything already,
what can I offer you?
Wander from shrine to shrine,
visit gods, look all over for fulfilment.
The further away you look
from your own self,
the greener seems
the next heap of grass.
The way is like an herb garden:
enclose it with silence, self-restraint,
and actions that follow these.

Then sacrifice everything you do,
like animals on the Mother's altar.
Gradually your whole crop
of deeds gets eaten, and
only emptiness remains.

—Lalla, 14th century CE, Kashmir.

Everybody Does Not See Alike

I feel that a person may be happy in this world.

I know that this world is a world of imagination and vision. I see everything I paint in this world, but everybody does not see alike.

To the eyes of a miser, a guinea is more beautiful than the sun, and a bag worn with the use of money has more beautiful proportions than a vine filled with grapes.

The tree that moves some to tears of joy is, in the eyes of others, only a green thing that stands in the way.

Some scarcely see nature at all. But to the eyes of the person of imagination, nature is imagination itself.

—William Blake, 1799 (Letter), England.

Like the Homesick Going Home

In the street and in society I am almost invariably cheap and dissipated, my life is unspeakably poor. No amount of gold or respectability would in the least redeem it—like dining with the governor or a member of Congress!

But alone in distant woods or fields, in unpretending sprout lands or pastures tracked by rabbits, even on a black and (to most) cheerless day like this, when a villager would be thinking of an inn, I come to myself. I once more feel myself grandly related, and that the cold and solitude are friends of mine.

I find this value equivalent to what others get by church-going and prayer. I come to my solitary, woodland walk as the homesick go home.

It is as if I always meet in those places some grand, serene, immortal, infinitely encouraging (though invisible) companion, and walk with it.

—Henry David Thoreau, 1857 (Journals), USA.

Returning to the Fields after Government Service

When I was young, I was out of tune with the herd.
My only love was for the hills and mountains.
Unwittingly I fell into the web of the world's dust
and was not free for the next thirty years.
The migrant bird longs for the old wood.
The fish captive in a tank thinks of its native pool.
I had rescued from wildness a patch of the southern moor
and, still rustic, I returned to field and garden.
My ground covers no more than ten acres.
My thatched cottage has eight or nine rooms.
Elms and willows cluster by the eaves.
Peach trees and plum trees grow before the hall.
Hazy, hazy—the distant hamlets of people.
Steady the smoke of the half-deserted village.
A dog barks somewhere in the deep lanes.
A cock crows at the top of the mulberry tree.
At gate and courtyard—no murmur of the world's dust.
In the empty rooms—leisure and deep stillness.
For a long time, I lived checked by the bars of a cage.
Now I have returned to nature and freedom.

—Tao Yuanming, 4th–5th century CE, China.

Returning to Nature from Jail

I hope to be at least a month with my friends, and to gain peace and balance, and a less troubled heart, and a sweeter mood. I have a strange longing for the great, simple primeval things, such as the sea—to me no less of a mother than the earth.

It seems to me that we all look at nature too much, and live with her too little. I discern great sanity in the Greek attitude. They never chattered about sunsets, or discussed whether the shadows on the grass were really mauve or not. But they saw that the sea was for the swimmer and the sand for the feet of the runner. They loved the trees for the shadow that they cast and the forest for its silence at noon. The vineyard-dressers wreathed their hair with ivy that they might keep off the rays of the sun as they stooped over the young shoots, and for the artist and the athlete—the two types that Greece gave us— they plaited with garlands the leaves of the bitter laurel and of the wild parsley, which otherwise had been of no service to them.

We call ours a utilitarian age, and we yet do not know the uses of any single thing. We have forgotten that water can cleanse, and fire purify, and that the earth is mother to us all.

As a consequence our art is of the moon and plays with shadows, while Greek art is of the sun and deals directly with things. I feel sure that in elemental forces there is purification, and I want to go back to them and live in their presence.

Society, as we have constituted it, will have no place for me, has none to offer. But nature, whose sweet rains fall on unjust and just alike, will have clefts in the rocks where I may hide, and secret valleys in whose silence I may weep undisturbed.

She will hang the night with stars so that I may walk abroad in the darkness without stumbling, and send the wind over my footprints so that none may track me to my hurt. She will cleanse me in great waters and with bitter herbs make me whole.

—Oscar Wilde, 1897, Ireland.

The Word Wilderness Should Not Lose Its Meaning

People find peace of mind and benefit for their souls in forests. In former times they used to retreat into thick forests and there, away from the idle emptiness of the everyday world, seek out their own salvation through prayer and work.

Just one look at the evergreen conifers of our homeland gladdens the eyes. It portrays a symbol of our hope for eternal life. Some people go to the deserts to look for the same thing.

The forests that surround our monasteries must be preserved from destruction by every means possible. We must prevent the word *wilderness* from losing its meaning altogether.

—Father Macarius of Optina,
18th–19th century, Russia.

The Real Words

A song of the rolling earth, and of words according:
Were you thinking that those were the words,
those upright lines, those curves, angles, dots?
No, those are not the words.
The substantial words are in the ground and sea.
They are in the air, they are in you.
Were you thinking that those were the words,
those delicious sounds out of your friends' mouths?
No, the real words are more delicious than that.
Human bodies are words, myriads of words.
In the best poems re-appears the body,
man's or woman's, well-shaped, natural, gay.
Every part able, active, receptive,
without shame or the need of shame.
Air, soil, water, fire—*those* are words.
I myself am a word with them—
my qualities interpenetrate with theirs.
My name is nothing to them.
Though it were said in three thousand languages,
what would air, soil, water, fire, know of my name?
The work of souls is by those inaudible words of the earth.
The earth does not withhold, it is generous enough.
The truths of the earth continually wait,
they are not so concealed either.
They are calm, subtle, intransmissible by print.

They are imbued through all things
conveying themselves willingly.
Whoever you are, you are he or she
for whom the earth is solid and liquid.
You are he or she
for whom the sun and moon hang in the sky.
For none more than you are the present and the past.
For none more than you is immortality.
Each man to himself and each woman to herself
is the word of the past and present
and the true word of immortality.
No one can acquire for another—not one.
Not one can grow for another—not one.
I swear the earth shall surely be complete
to him or her who shall be complete.
The earth remains jagged and broken
only to him or her who remains jagged and broken.
I swear there is no greatness or power
that does not emulate those of the earth.
There can be no theory of any account
unless it corroborate the theory of the earth.
No politics, song, religion, behavior,
or what not is of account
unless it compare with
the amplitude of the earth.
Unless it face the exactness, vitality,
impartiality, rectitude of the earth.

I swear I begin to see little or nothing
in audible words.
All merges toward the presentation
of the unspoken meanings of the earth,
toward the one who sings the songs of the body
and of the truths of the earth.
Toward the one who makes
dictionaries of words
that print cannot touch.

—Walt Whitman, 1855–1892 (*Leaves of Grass*), USA.

The Breath of the Reed

The breath of the reed is the very voice of solitude.

Shrill and clear and passionless it rose to the temple gate, borne on deep waves of mountain air that were perfumed with flowers and colored with the rays of the low sun.

People had come and gone, life had surged up the flanks of the hills and retreated again, leaving the old gods to resume their sway over rock and flowering thorn, in peace and loneliness and beauty.

> —Gertrude Bell, 1907 (*The Desert and the Sown: Travels in Palestine and Syria*), England.

A Rock by the Pondside

What is the relation between a bird and the ear that appreciates its melody, to whom, perchance, it is more charming and significant than to anyone else?

Certainly they are intimately related, and the one was made for the other. It is a natural fact.

If I were to discover that a certain kind of stone by the pond-shore was affected, say partially disintegrated, by a particular natural sound, as of a bird or insect, I see that one could not be completely described without describing the other.

I am that rock by the pondside.

—Henry David Thoreau, 1857 (Journals), USA.

8

Wild to the End

Snow Falling in a River

One moment I saw a river flowing gently.
The next, all bridges washed away.
One moment I saw a bush flowering.
The next I saw no rose or thorn—just branches.
One moment I saw a cooking fire blazing.
The next just ashes, no fire nor smoke.
Pleasures spread like poppies.
You seize the flower, the blossom drops.
We are like snow falling in a river—
a moment white, then melted forever.
I don't trust what is
being said through me—
not for a moment!
Still I drink the wine of my own words,
then I seize the darkness that arises and
tear it into little pieces.
As the moon wanes,
I find a mad person roaming inside,
longing for the Beloved.
I call out to soothe her pain—
'It is I, Lalla . . . I!"
The Beloved appears, and
all further sensing and doing
disappear.

—Lalla, 14th century CE, Kashmir.

Death and Life and Beauty

One is constantly reminded of the infinite lavishness and fertility of nature—inexhaustible abundance amid what seems enormous waste.

And yet when we look into any of her operations that lie within reach of our minds, we learn that no particle of her material is wasted or worn out. It is eternally flowing from use to use, beauty to yet higher beauty.

We soon cease to lament waste and death, and rather rejoice and exult in the imperishable, un-spendable wealth of the universe, and faithfully watch and wait the reappearance of everything that melts and fades and dies about us, feeling sure that its next appearance will be better and more beautiful than the last.

On no subject are our ideas more warped and pitiable than on death. Let children walk with nature, let them see the beautiful blendings and communions of death and life, their joyous inseparable unity, as taught in woods and meadows, plains and mountains and streams of our blessed star. They will learn that death is stingless indeed, and as beautiful as life, and that the grave has no victory, for it never fights. All is divine harmony.

—John Muir, 1869 (*My First Summer in the Sierra*),
1916 (*A Thousand-Mile Walk to the Gulf*), Scotland-USA.

The Shadow of the Bamboo in the Moonlight

When you look at a dead man's face, there is no action in it, but he is not resting either. He is in eternal life. He is living. He has not gone when he dies. He has neither come nor gone. There is no beginning, no end. Therefore, there is no coming or going. And from the state of Reality, there is neither right nor wrong. Nothing is standing or walking.

The shadow of the bamboo in the moonlight is sweeping the dust from the stairs all night long, but nothing has happened. No dust has been swept. No stairs have been swept. From the standpoint of Reality, nothing has happened. Not a mote of dust has been swept. We came here. We lived. We died. Nothing has happened. Originally, from the standpoint of Reality, this is the bottom of the empty sea.

—Sokei-an Sasaki, 1935–39 (Lectures), Japan-USA.

Beyond?

I don't love the Christian conceptions of a beyond, and I increasingly move away from them without, of course, thinking of attacking them. They may have their right to exist like so many other hypotheses of the divine periphery.

For me, however, they present above all the danger of rendering our lost ones less concrete and initially less reachable. And when we move ourselves longingly toward this beyond and away from here, we are also rendered less precise, less earthly: a condition that for now and as long as we are here and related to tree, flower, and soil, we have yet to embrace purely and even yet still to attain!

—Rainer Maria Rilke, 1923, Austria-Bohemia
(now Czech Republic).

An Old Age Dream of Climbing Mountains

At night in my dream I bravely climbed a mountain,
going out alone with my staff of holly wood.
A thousand crags, a hundred hundred valleys—
in my dream-journey none were unexplored,
and all the while my feet never grew tired,
and my step was as strong as in my young days.
Can it be that when the mind travels backward
the body also returns to its old state?
And can it be, as between body and soul,
that the body may diminish while the soul is still strong?
Soul and body—both are vanities.
Dreaming and waking—both alike unreal.
During the day my feet are weak and tottering.
In the night my steps go striding over the hills.
Since day and night are divided in equal parts,
between the two I get as much as I lose.

> —Bai Juyi, 8th–9th century CE, China (written
> when he was over seventy).

Wind in the Woods

The cricket, the gurgling stream, the rushing wind amid the trees—all speak to me soberly yet encouragingly of the steady onward progress of the universe. My heart leaps into my mouth at the sound of the wind in the woods.

I, whose life was but yesterday so desultory and shallow, suddenly recover my spirits, my spirituality, through my hearing. I see a goldfinch go twittering through the still, overcast day and am reminded of the peeping flocks that will soon herald the thoughtful season.

Ah! If I could live so that there should be no desultory moment in all my life! That in the trivial season, when small fruits are ripe, my fruits might be ripe also. That I could always match nature with my moods. That in each season, when some part of nature especially flourishes, then a corresponding part of me would also flourish.

Ah, I would walk, I would sit and sleep, with natural piety! What if I could pray aloud or silently, as I went along by the brooksides, pray a cheerful prayer like the birds?

For joy I could embrace the earth. I shall delight to be buried in it.

I sometimes feel as if I were rewarded merely for expecting better hours. I did not despair of worthier moods, and now I have occasion to be grateful for the flood of life that is flowing over me.

—Henry David Thoreau, 1851 (Journals), USA

Substance, Shadow, Spirit

High and low, wise and simple—
everyone busily hoards up
the moments of life.
What a mistake!
I have exposed the bitter side of
amassing the products of both
our substance and our shadow,
the seen and unseen effects of life.
Then I made spirit instruct them both
how to follow nature's way
and dissolve this bitterness.
Substance speaks to Its Shadow:
Heaven and earth exist forever.
Mountains and rivers never change.
But herbs and trees constantly rotate,
renovated and withered by the dews and frosts.
And humanity—the wise, the divine—
shall we alone escape this law?
By chance we appear in the world for a moment
then suddenly depart, never to return.
How can we know that the friends we have left
are missing us or even thinking of us?
Only the objects that we used remain.
Friends see them and their tears flow.
No magical arts can save me.

Though you may hope for a wizard's help,
I beg you to listen to this advice:
When you can get wine, drink it.
Shadow replies to Substance:
Yes, drugs of immortality are just
foolish tools—no way to preserve life.
I would gladly wander in paradise,
but it is far away, and I don't know the road.
Since the day I was joined to you, my substance,
we have shared all our joys and pains.
While you rested in the shade, I left you awhile,
but until the end we exist together.
Yet this sharing won't last, sadly,
and we shall slip away, still together.
But I disagree that the body's decay
means our reputation also departs—
a thought unendurable, it burns the heart.
Let's strive and work while we can
to do something that people will praise.
Maybe wine will relieve our sorrow, but
how can you compare it with lasting fame?
Spirit clarifies:
Heaven can only set things in motion,
not control the things it has made.
Humanity, the second of the Three Realms,
owes its priority to me.
Though I am different from you both,

we were born entwined, we can't escape
life's intimate sharing of good and evil.
The Three Emperors[1] were demigods.
Yet today—where are they?
Peng[2] lived to a great age,
yet departed at last, still longing to stay.
Sooner or later, we all go,
wise or simple—no reprieve.
Wine may bring forgetfulness,
but doesn't it hasten old age?
And if you set your heart
on being remembered,
can you count on anyone praising you?
Too much thinking—you injure me!
Better just go where fate leads:
drift on the stream of constant flow,
without joy, without fear.
When you must go, then go,
and make as little fuss as you can.

—Tao Yuanming, 4th–5th century CE, China.

---

1 In Chinese mythology, the Three Emperors or Three Sovereigns were
considered god-kings or demigods who taught humanity essential skills,
like use of fire and farming.
2 A Chinese god of longevity, said to have lived 800 years.

Being Worked

I, Lalla, began in the hope of blooming like a cotton flower, but the cleaner and the carder of the fiber had other ideas and gave me many kicks and hits.

The spinner lifted me from the turning wheel all gossamer, yet I received one more beating in the weaver's workroom.

The washer turned me over and over, hitting me on a stone, rubbing me with fuller's earth and soap.

Finally, the tailor's scissors cut me into pieces, thread stitched me together.

Only then did I obtain the way of the supreme.

I came into this universe of birth and rebirth. Through long practice I gained the light of knowledge.

If anyone dies, it's not my business, and if I die, it's nothing to them.

It's good if I die, and good if I continue to live.

—Lalla, 14th century CE, Kashmir.

Journey into Being

I believe that I now understand in some small measure why the Buddhist goes on pilgrimage to a mountain. The journey is itself part of the technique by which the god is sought. It is a journey into Being. For as I penetrate more deeply into the mountain's life, I penetrate also into my own.

For an hour I am beyond desire. It is not ecstasy, that leap out of the self that makes man like a god. I am not out of myself, but in myself. I am.

To know Being, this is the final grace accorded from the mountain.

—Nan Shepherd, 1947
(*The Living Mountain*), Scotland.

The Flight of the Monarchs

For me it was one of the loveliest of the summer's hours, and all the details will remain in my memory: that blue September sky, the sounds of wind in the spruces and surf on the rocks, the gulls busy with their foraging, alighting with deliberate grace, the distant views of Griffiths Head and Todd Point, today so clearly etched, though once half seen in swirling fog. But most of all I shall remember the Monarchs, that unhurried westward drift of one small winged form after another, each drawn by some invisible force. We talked a little about their migration, their life history. Did they return? We thought not; for most, at least, this was the closing journey of their lives.

But it occurred to me this afternoon, remembering, that it had been a happy spectacle, that we had felt no sadness when we spoke of the fact that there would be no return. And rightly—for when any living thing has come to the end of its life cycle we accept that end as natural.

For the Monarch, that cycle is measured in a known span of months. For ourselves, the measure is something else, the span of which we cannot know. But the thought is the same: when that intangible cycle has run its course it is a natural and not unhappy thing that a life comes to its end.

That is what those brightly fluttering bits of life taught me this morning. I found a deep happiness in it—so, I hope, may you. Thank you for this morning.

—Rachel Carson, 1963 (last letter to a friend after a visit to the shore near the mouth of the Sheepscot River in Maine), USA.

ACKNOWLEDGMENTS

Canongate Books Ltd, Edinburgh, Scotland, for permission to reprint an excerpt from *The Living Mountain* by Nan Shepherd from *The Grampian Quartet: The Quarry Wood, The Weatherhouse, A Pass in the Grampians, The Living Mountain.* Copyright Sheila M. Clouston 1928, 1930, 1933, 1977. Reprinted by permission.

Frances Collin, Trustee, for permission to reprint excerpts from *Lost Woods: The Discovered Writing of Rachel Carson.* Edited by Linda Lear. Published by Beacon Press. Copyright 1998 by Roger Allen Christie. Reprinted by permission of Frances Collin, Trustee.

Jennifer Ferraro and White Cloud Press for permission to reprint "The Teaching of the Running River" from *Quarreling with God: Mystic Rebel Poems of the Dervishes of Turkey.* Copyright 2007 Jennifer Ferraro. *www.whitecloudpress.com*

First Zen Institute for permission to reprint excerpts from *Original Nature: Zen Comments on the Sixth Patriarch's Platform Sutra* by Sokei-an Sasaki. Copyright First Zen Institute 2012. And from *Zen Pivots: Lectures on Buddhism and Zen.* Copyright First Zen Institute 1998. *www.firstzen.org*

Bradley Jersak and Freshwind Press for permission to reprint a selection from *Awaiting God: A New Translation* by Simone Weil (2012). *https://bradjersak.com*

Nicholas R. Martin for permission to reprint excerpts from the new Arabic translation of *The Processions: Al-Mawakib*, by Kahlil Gibran, pp. 55, 65, 66, 67, 70 (print edition). Copyright 2014 Nicholas R. Martin. The excerpts here appear in various parts of the text, which takes the form of a conversation between two voices.

Penguin Random House for permission to reprint excerpts from *The Poet's Guide to Life: The Wisdom of Rilke* by Rainer Maria Rilke, edited and translated by Ulrich Baer, copyright 2005 by Ulrich Baer. Used by permission of Modern Library, an imprint of Random House, a division of Penguin Random House LLC. All rights reserved.

Suhrkamp Verlag, for permission to reprint excerpts from *Wanderung: Aufzeichnungen* by Hermann Hesse. Copyright Insel Verlag 2015. This selection from the S. Fischer-Verlag printing of 1920.

Appendix

VOICES OF THE WILD

(Note: For Chinese names, the family or surname appears first.)

Fariduddin Attar (1145–1221), Persian poet and pharmacist who wrote a history of the early Sufi saints and mystics, as well as the epic poem *Mantiq-u-Tayr* ("The Conference of the Birds"), about a journey of birds to find their king. The excerpt is adapted from the Edward FitzGerald translation of the poem.

Baal Shem Tov (Israel ben Eliezer, 1698–1760), Polish mystical rabbi, regarded as the founder of Hasidic Judaism. His central teaching was direct connection with the divine (*dvekut*), which he felt was present in every facet of daily life rather than only in acts of religious ritual.

Bai Juyi (also known as Po Chu-i, 772–846 CE), Chinese Tang Dynasty poet. Living through the reign of eight different emperors, he was governor of three different provinces, an occupational hazard that influenced his poetry and social criticism.

Gertrude Bell (1868–1926), English writer, translator, traveler, explorer, archaeologist who traveled extensively in pre-WWI Syria, Mesopotamia, Asia Minor, and Arabia. The included excerpts come from *The Desert and the Sown: Travels in Palestine and Syria* (1907). See the online Gertrude Bell Archive at Newcastle (UK) University: *www.gerty.ncl.ac.uk*

William Blake (1757–1827), English mystic, poet, painter, and printmaker, best known for his "Songs of Innocence and Experience" and "The Marriage of Heaven and Hell." Considered mad by his contemporaries, he became famous only after his death. See *www.blakesociety.org*

Rachel Carson (1907–1964), American marine biologist and conservationist, best known for her multiple books about the sea as well as her early environmental critique *Silent Spring* (1962), which exposed the danger of the use of synthetic pesticides, widely used at the time. See: *http://www.rachelcarson.org*

Chuang Tzu (also known as Zhuang Zhou), 4th-century BCE China, credited with writing one of the classics of Taoism, the *Zhuangzi*. See, for instance: *taoism.net*

Emily Dickinson (1830–1886), American poet, almost unknown during her lifetime, now considered one of the great American poets of the 19th century. She authored nearly 1800 poems, all untitled, only a dozen of which were published during her lifetime. See: Dickinson Electronic Archives: *www.emilydickinson.org*

Kahlil Gibran (Gibran Khalil Gibran, 1883–1931), Lebanese-American poet, artist, and political writer, best known for his book *The Prophet* (1923). The excerpt here is from one of his lesser-known Arabic language works, "The Processions," in a new translation. See *leb.net/gibran/*

Shah Hatayi (Shah Ismail I, 1487–1524), Azerbaijani-Persian founder of the Safavid Dynasty and poet, who wrote in the Azerbaijani and Persian languages. A large body of Alevi and Bektashi Sufi poetry has been attributed to him.

Hermann Hesse (1877–1962), German-Swiss poet, novelist, and painter whose best-known works include *Siddhartha* and *The Glass Bead Game.* He wrote the book *Wandering* during an extended hike through the Swiss mountains in 1917–1918. See: Hermann Hesse Page (English/German): *hesse.projects.gss. ucsb.edu*

Palladius Hieronymous, 4th–5th century CE monk from Galatia (in present day Turkey) who visited many of the desert fathers in Egypt and compiled their stories and sayings in a Syriac language history entitled *Paradise.* According to one commentator, the word he used for the title actually means "garden" and "the monks themselves were the flowers of the garden of God." The stories here are rendered from the 1904 English version of E. A. W. Budge (see bibliography).

Oliver Wendell Holmes (1809–1894), American physician, poet, and author, contemporary and friend of Ralph Waldo

Emerson and Henry Longfellow. Best known for his book *The Autocrat of the Breakfast-Table* (1858), from which the included excerpt comes.

Hsieh Tao-yün, 4th-century CE Chinese poet, niece of a politician and wife of the general Wang Ning-chih. According to one of her translators, "The general was so stupid that she finally deserted him." What little is known about her life is contained in the *Shih-shuo hsin-yu* ("A New Account of the Tales of the World"), which collected anecdotes about life in the elite circles of the late Han dynasty and Wei-Chin period, about 150–420 CE.

Ilias the Presbyter, 11th-century CE lawyer from Constantinople (now Istanbul in Turkey) who became an orthodox Christian priest. Little is known about his life, although his writings are included in the *Philokalia*, a collection of texts from the contemplative *hesychast* ("stillness") tradition.

Isaac of Nineveh (circa 613–700 CE), from Eastern Arabia, early bishop and theologian of the Aramaic-speaking church, later recognized as a saint in both the Syrian Orthodox Church and the Assyrian Church of the East.

Lalla ("Laleshwari," or "Lal Ded," 1320–1392), Kashmiri mystic and poet, her verses are some of the earliest compositions in the Kashmiri language. Today she is claimed by both the Hindu and Muslim traditions (reflecting the conflicted political situation in Kashmir), but during her life, she embraced and transcended both. Selections here are my versions rendered from the 1920 translations of Grierson and Barnett (see bibliography).

Lao Tze (also Laozi, literally "old master), 6th-century BCE semi-legendary Chinese philosopher and poet, to whom is traditionally attributed the authorship of the *Tao Te Ching*.

Thomas Edward (T. E.) Lawrence (1888–1935), British archaeologist, army officer, diplomat, and writer, who became famous as "Lawrence of Arabia" for his work as a British liaison to the revolt of Arab tribes against the Ottoman Empire in WWI. See T. E. Lawrence Society: *telsociety.org.uk*

Li Bai (701–762 CE), one of the foremost poets of the Chinese Tang dynasty, he composed more than a thousand poems, which embraced nature, dreams, everyday life, and current events.

Lie Yukou, 4th-century BCE Chinese philosopher and author of the Taoist classic book the *Liezi*. During the reign of the Emperor Xuanzong of the Tang dynasty, the *Liezi* was renowned along with the more famous *Tao Te Ching* and *Zuangzi* texts.

Abba Macarius of Egypt (300–391 CE), desert solitary and priest who lived in the Egyptian Western desert around Wadi El Natrun, known in Christian literature as "Scete." For a while he was exiled by Roman Emperor Valens during a dispute over the Nicene Creed.

Macarius of Optina, 1788–1860, Russian monk and elder of the forest hermit community of Optina Pustina, near Kozelsk in the Kaluga region.

Meister Eckhart (Eckhart von Hochheim, 1260–1328), German theologian and mystic, known for his eccentric yet practical sermons in vernacular German, tried as a heretic by Pope John XXII. The selection included is my translation from the German.

Jetsun Milarepa (1028–1111), Tibetan Buddhist yogi and poet, who according to Tibetan history was a sorcerer and murderer in his youth, becoming enlightened after many austerities assigned by his teacher Marpa.

Edna St. Vincent Millay (1892–1950), American poet, playwright, early feminist activist. Posthumously named by the Equality Forum as one of the thirty-one icons of the 2015 LGBT History Month.

John Muir (1838–1914), Scottish-American naturalist, author, environmental philosopher, cofounder of the Sierra Club, early advocate for the preservation of wilderness areas in the USA. The excerpts here are from his many journals, magazine articles, and books written during a long life of travel and exploration.

Rabbi Nachman of Bratslav (1772–1810), founder of the Breslov Hasidic movement and a grandson of the Hasidic mystic the Baal Shem Tov. He is best known for his teaching stories. He famously said, "all the world is a very narrow bridge, but the main thing is to have no fear at all."

Marguerite Porete, 13th-century French mystic, author of *The Mirror of Simple Souls*, whose theme is the many expressions and workings of divine love. The book is now seen as one of the principal texts of the medieval heresy labeled the "Free Spirits," and Porete was burned at the stake in 1310 after refusing to recant her views.

Rabia al-Adawiyya al Qaysiyya (Rabi'ah al-Basri), 8th-century CE Iraqi Sufi saint, one of the best known of the early Sufi women mystics. The stories retold here are from Fariduddin Attar's hagiographical collection *Tazkirat al-Awliya* ("Biographies of the Saints").

Rainer Maria Rilke (1875–1926), Austrian-Czech poet and novelist, best known for his poetry collections *Sonnets to Orpheus* and *Duino Elegies*. The excerpts here are from a new translation of his selected correspondence on work, nature, language, art, illness, solitude, and other subjects. (See the Bibliography for reference.)

Jelaluddin Rumi ("Jalal ad-Din Muhammad Balkhi," 1207–1273), Persian Sufi mystic and poet, best known for his *Mathnawi*, a multivolume collection of poetic stories, teachings and Qur'anic interpretations, often called "the Qur'an in

Persian." The selections included are my versions from previous literal ones. See, among others: *www.dar-al-masnavi.org*

Saadi Shirazi (Muslih al-Din Abdallah Shirazi, 1210–1291 approx.), Persian poet, writer, storyteller, and humorist. He traveled widely during his life and spent time with farmers, merchants, preachers, travelers, thieves, and Sufi dervishes, all of whose views and unique ways of speaking are reflected in his two works *Golistan* ("The Rose Garden") and *Bustan* ("The Orchard").

Amma Sara ("Sara of the Desert"), 5th-century CE Christian "desert mother," known only through the "Sayings of the Desert Fathers" (*Apophthegmanta Patrum*) originally passed down orally then translated in various collections.

Sokei-An Sasaki (1882–1945), Japanese Rinzai monk who founded the First Zen Institute of America in New York City. Coming to California in 1906, Sokei-An traveled throughout North America, often doing odd jobs, before moving to New York City in 1916, where he began to give classes and lectures on Zen. The included selections are from his long oral commentary on the famous "Sutra of the Sixth Patriarch" and from other talks offered in his small Manhattan apartment (see Bibliogaphy). See: First Zen Institute, *www.firstzen.org*

Nan Shepherd (1893–1981), Scottish poet and writer, author of three novels and one nonfiction book on her experiences hiking in the Cairngorm Mountains near her home. She wrote

The Living Mountain in 1947 but chose not to publish it for thirty years. Excerpts here are from this work. She is currently commemorated on one of the Scottish £5 banknotes.

Abba Sisoes (Sisoes of Scete), 5th-century CE Christian solitary and ascetic who spent sixty years in the Egyptian Western desert around Wadi El Natrun, known in Christian literature as "Scete."

Amma Syncletica of Alexandria, 4th-century CE Christian "desert mother." Daughter of wealthy parents, upon their death, she gave away all of her belongings and along with her sister became a hermit.

Tao Yuanming (Tao Qian, c. 365–427 CE), Chinese poet who retired from civil service to spend the rest of his life in seclusion. Both his father and grandfather had served as government officials, but Tao Yuanming rebelled against the corruption prevalent in the Jin Dynasty court. He is considered a foremost exemplar of "Field and Gardens" poetry, the favorite themes of which were farming and drinking. Versions here are adapted from the 1919 translations of Arthur Waley.

Henry David Thoreau (1817–1862), American transcendentalist poet, essayist, and philosopher, best known for his book *Walden* (1854) and his essay "Civil Disobedience" (1849). For his complete works see *www.thoreausociety.org*

Mark Twain (Samuel L. Clemens, 1835–1910), American writer, humorist, lecturer, storyteller, best known for his novel *The Adventures of Huckleberry Finn*. The excerpt here is from his book *Life on the Mississippi* (1883), which describes his time as a young pilot on a Mississippi River steamboat before the Civil War. Many sites, including: *www.marktwainproject.org*

Varsonofy of Optina (1845–1913), Russian orthodox priest, spiritual writer, and one of the elders of the Optina Pustina, a forest hermit community and monastery near Kozelsk in the Kaluga region. See: *www.optina.ru/* (Russian language site)

Vijnana Bhairava Tantra, a mystical text from the tradition of Kashmiri Shaivism that unfolds as a discourse between the god Bhairava (a manifestation of Shiva) and Bhairavi (Shakti). It presents 112 tantric methods of becoming one with the most profound reality. Estimates of age differ, but it dates from at least the 12th century CE and perhaps as old as the 5th century BCE. The text was popularized in a version in *Zen Flesh, Zen Bones* by Paul Reps and Nyogen Senzaki in 1957.

Simone Weil (1909–1943), French philosopher, political activist, and mystic, most of whose work was not published until after her death. The selection here is from a new translation of her book *Awaiting God* by Bradley Jersak. See *bradjersak.com*

Walt Whitman (1819–1892), American poet, essayist, and journalist, sometimes called the "father of free verse." Best known for his collection *Leaves of Grass*, revised over a thirty-seven-year period, from which the excerpt here of "A Song of the Rolling Earth" comes. See: *whitmanarchive.org*

Oscar Wilde (1854–1900), Irish poet, novelist, and playwright, author of *The Picture of Dorian Gray, The Importance of Being Earnest,* and *Salomé.* At the height of his success, he was arrested and sentenced to two years' hard labor in a London prison for homosexual behavior. The excerpt in the final section is from *De Profundis* ("from the depths") 1905, a letter written to his former lover "Bosie," Lord Alfred Douglas. After being released, Wilde left for France and died there three years later.

BIBLIOGRAPHY AND
RECOMMENDED READING

Alexander, G. G., et al. (1917). *Sacred Books and Early Literature of the East: Medieval China*. New York, London: Parke, Austin, and Lipscomb.

Arberry, A. J. (1979). *Muslim Saints and Mystics: Episodes from the Tadhkirat al-Auliya ("Memorial of the Saints") by Farid al-Din Attar*. London: Routlege & Kegan Paul.

Bell, Gertrude (1907). *The Desert and the Sown: Travels in Palestine and Syria*. London: William Heinemann.

Bowden, Emily F. (1906). *The Fathers of the Desert, Volumes One and Two*. London: Burns and Oats.

Brock, Sebastian P., and Susan Ashbrook Harvey (1998). *Holy Women of the Syrian Orient*. Berkeley: University of California Press.

Buber, Martin (1956). *The Tales of Rabbi Nachman*. New York: Horizon Press.

Budge, E. A. Wallis (1904). *The Book of Paradise, Being the Histories and Sayings of the Monks and Ascetics of the Egyptian*

Desert by Palladius Hieronymus and Others. London: Lady Meux.

Carson, Rachel (1998). *Lost Woods: The Discovered Writing of Rachel Carson*. Edited by Linda Lear. Boston: Beacon Press.

Colegate, Isabel (2003). *A Pelican in the Wilderness: Hermits, Solitaries and Recluses*. London: HarperCollins.

Cornell, Rkia, trans. (1999). *Early Sufi Women: Dhikr an-Niswa al-Mta'abbidat as-Sufiyyat* by Abu Abd Ar-Rahman As-Sulami. Louisville, KY: Fons Vitae.

Dickinson, Emily (1955). *The Complete Poems of Emily Dickinson*. Edited by Thomas H. Johnson. Delhi: Kalyani Publishers.

Ferraro, Jennifer, and Latif Bolat, trans. (2007). *Quarreling with God: Mystic Rebel Poems of the Dervishes of Turkey*. Ashland, OR: White Cloud Press.

FitzGerald, Edward (1889). *Bird Parliament by Farid ud-din Attar*. London, New York: Macmillan and Company.

Gibran, Kahlil (2014). *The Processions: Al-Mawakib*. Translation by Abdullah Halawani. Nicholas Martin, Editor. Digital Edition. Copyright Nicholas R. M. Martin 2014.

Grierson, George, and Lionel Barnett (1920). *Lalla-Vakyani or the Wise Sayings of Lal Ded, A Mystic Poetess of Ancient Kashmir*. London: Royal Asiatic Society.

Hesse, Hermann (1920). *Wanderung: Aufzeichnungen von Hermann Hesse.* Berlin: S. Fischer Verlag.

Kirchberger, Clare, ed. (1927). *The Mirror of Simple Souls.* London: Burns, Oates, and Washbourne, Ltd.

Lawrence, T. E. (1922). *Seven Pillars of Wisdom.* Harmondsworth, UK: Penguin Books.

Lawrence, T. E. (1927). *Revolt in the Desert.* London: Jonathan Cape.

Legge, James, et al. (1917). *Sacred Books and Early Literature of the East: Ancient China.* New York, London: Parke, Austin, and Lipscomb.

Quint, Josef (1979). *Meister Eckhart: Deutsche Predigten und Traktate.* Zurich: Diogenes Verlag.

Rilke, Rainer Maria (2005). *The Poet's Guide to Life: The Wisdom of Rilke,* edited and translated by Ulrich Baer. New York: Penguin Random House.

Sasaki, Sokei-An (1998). *Zen Pivots: Lectures on Buddhism and Zen.* Edited by Mary Farkas and Robert Lopez. New York: Weatherhill.

Sasaki, Sokei-An (2012). *Original Nature: Zen Comments on the Sixth Patriarch's Platform Sutra.* New York: First Zen Institute.

Shepherd, Nan (1996). *The Grampian Quartet: The Quarry Wood, The Weatherhouse, A Pass in the Grampians, The Living Mountain*. Edinburgh, London: Canongate.

Smith, Margaret (1994). *Readings from the Mystics of Islam*. Westport, CT: Pir Publications.

St. Vincent Millay, Edna (1917). *Renascence and Other Poems*. New York, London: Harper and Brothers Publishers.

St. Vincent Millay, Edna (1921). *Second April*. New York: Mitchell Kennerley.

Swan, Laura (2001). *The Forgotten Desert Mothers: Sayings, Lives, and Stories of Early Christian Women*. New York, Mahwah, NJ: Paulist Press.

Thoreau, Henry David (1906). *The Writings of Henry David Thoreau* (multiple volumes). Boston, New York: Houghton Mifflin.

Thoreau, Henry David (1937). *Walden and Other Writings of Henry David Thoreau*. New York: The Modern Library.

Twain, Mark (1883). *Life on the Mississippi*. Boston: James R. Osgood and Company.

Waley, Arthur, trans. (1918). *A Hundred and Seventy Chinese Poems*. London: Constable and Company Ltd.

Waley, Arthur, trans. (1919). *More Translations from the Chinese*. London: George Allen and Unwin.

Waley, Arthur (1919). *The Poet Li Po, A.D. 701–762*. London: East and West, Ltd.

Weil, Simone (2012). *Awaiting God: A New Translation of Attente de Dieu* and *Lettre a un Religieux by Simone Weil*, translated by Bradley Jersak. Abbotsford, Canada: Freshwind Press.

Wensinck, A. J. (1923). *Mystic Treatises by Isaac of Nineveh*. Amsterdam: Uitgave Der Koninklijke Akademie Van Wetenschappen.

Whinfield, E. H., et al. (1917). *Sacred Books and Early Literature of the East: Medieval Persia*. New York, London: Parke, Austin, and Lipscomb.

Wolpé, Sholeh (2017). *The Conference of the Birds: Attar*. New York, London: W. W. Norton and Company.

ABOUT THE EDITOR
AND TRANSLATOR

Neil Douglas-Klotz, PhD, is a renowned writer in the fields of Middle Eastern spirituality and the translation and interpretation of the ancient Semitic languages of Hebrew, Aramaic, and Arabic. Living in Scotland, he directs the Edinburgh Institute for Advanced Learning and for many years was co-chair of the Mysticism Group of the American Academy of Religion.

A frequent speaker and workshop leader, he is the author of several books. His books on the Aramaic spirituality of Jesus include *Prayers of the Cosmos*, *The Hidden Gospel*, *Original Meditation: The Aramaic Jesus and the Spirituality of Creation*, and *Blessings of the Cosmos*. His books on a comparative view of "native" Middle Eastern spirituality include *Desert Wisdom: A Nomad's Guide to Life's Big Questions* and *The Tent of Abraham* (with Rabbi Arthur Waskow and Sr. Joan Chittister). His books on Sufi spirituality include *The Sufi Book of Life: 99 Pathways of the Heart for the Modern Dervish* and *The Little Book of Sufi Stories*. His biographical collections of the works of his Sufi teachers include *Gardens of Vision and Initiation* (Samuel L. Lewis) and *Illuminating the Shadow* (Moineddin Jablonski). He has also written a mystery novel set in the first century C.E. Holy Land entitled *A Murder at Armageddon*.

He recently edited four "Little Books" published by Hampton Roads devoted to a new selection of the work of Lebanese-American writer, poet, and painter Kahlil Gibran, based on his Middle Eastern roots and culture.

For more information about his work, see the website of the Abwoon Network (*www.abwoon.org*) or visit his Facebook page (*www.facebook.com/AuthorNeilDouglasKlotz/*).

Also by Neil Douglas-Klotz
from Hampton Roads

Kahlil Gibran's Little Book of Life

Kahlil Gibran's Little Book of Love

Kahlil Gibran's Little Book of Secrets

Kahlil Gibran's Little Book of Wisdom

The Little Book of Sufi Stories:
Ancient Wisdom to Nourish the Heart

HAMPTON ROADS
PUBLISHING COMPANY

. . . for the evolving human spirit

Hampton Roads Publishing Company publishes books on a variety of subjects, including spirituality, health, and other related topics.

For a copy of our latest trade catalog, call (978) 465-0504 or visit our distributor's website at *www.redwheelweiser.com*. You can also sign up for our newsletter and special offers by going to *www.redwheelweiser.com/newsletter/*.